Reason to Believe

—

Mario Cuomo

Simon & Schuster

New York   London   Toronto   Sydney   Tokyo   Singapore

SIMON & SCHUSTER
Rockefeller Center
1230 Avenue of the Americas
New York, NY 10020

SIMON & SCHUSTER and colophon are registered trademarks
of Simon & Schuster Inc.

Designed by Levavi & Levavi

Manufactured in the United States of America

1   3   5   7   9   10   8   6   4   2

Library of Congress Cataloging-in-Publication Data

Cuomo, Mario Matthew.
Reason to believe / Mario Cuomo.
p. cm.
Includes index.
1. United States — Politics and government — 1993- 2. United
States — Economic policy — 1993- 3. United States — Social policy — 1993-
4. Republican Party (U.S. : 1854-) 5. Liberalism — United States.
I. Title.
JK271.C88 1995   95-39865   CIP
ISBN 0-684-81517-6

Contents

___

1

Where We Are and Where We're Going

———

This book is about where we are, where we're going, and what we should do about it.

As one who had been capsized by the Republican tide of 1994 and could no longer claim the authority bestowed by an election, I was hoping that a great chorus of voices would rise up to say what seemed to me so clear: "Of course the middle class, and most of America for that matter, has been unhappy with the direction this country was taking, but the new conservative Republican agenda won't solve our problems. It is a New Harshness that will make them worse, while stirring our meanest instincts and trampling upon our best impulses. It will hurt people, deny us opportunities, and damage America."

The chorus, however, has been slow to assemble. Probably because of that and because I had been in the middle of our political activities for a while, I began to receive invitations to speak and write on the subject. As I thought about these problems, I was reminded that the soul of this miraculous country has developed in two phases: the first, 150 years during which our staunch individualism was reflected in our laissez-faire government, and the second, the last six decades during which we created a modern America by learning to use our common resources more intelligently. My life and that second stage have overlapped almost exactly, and that, I think, has given me a special perspective on what is happening around us now.

With what seems a sudden spasm, America has been shoved onto a new political course that heads us backward toward our nation's first century, while the new crew yells to us, "That's where we'll find the future!"

Actually, the change wasn't so sudden. Over the last two decades, our middle class—the people not rich enough to be worry-free but not poor enough to be on welfare—has been growing increasingly restive. The American Dream seemed to be fading. Global competition, the new demands of rapidly exploding technology, the weakness of labor unions, and an internationally mobile American entrepreneurship were destroying our easy assumption that every generation of Americans would do better than the one before it. America was no longer the unchallenged economic colossus it had been for a quarter of a century after World War II. Good jobs with steadily rising wages were becoming more elusive. It was harder to raise a family securely than it had been for my generation in the 1950s and 1960s . . . and nearly impossible to do it on one average income.

In the 1990s, we've watched a new syndrome develop: an economy that is very good for investors but punishing to our workers with moderate or low skills.

At the same time that the economic future has grown bleaker for these workers, the culture around us has deteriorated. Drug use has created a new madness, especially among the poorest Americans jammed into ghettos without decent housing, schoolrooms, hospital beds, or jobs. Across the country hundreds of urban neighborhoods are now breeding places for a grotesque cluster of social pathologies—addiction; crime; constant, explosive violence; broken families; generations on welfare—an immense human tragedy. The economic impact of this social catastrophe has been vivid as well, and it's been all too easy for some politicians and commentators to exploit the notion that the middle class is paying much of that bill. Cynics, pandering to our basest instincts, have recently gone further and prodded this already anxious and embittered part of our people to turn their anger against the most vulnerable among us—welfare mothers, immigrants, people who look like the kind of people who live in ghettos—castigating them as the authors of their own misery and ours.

Altogether, a good portion of the $30,000-a-year factory workers and others caught up in the downsizing adjustments to a new, fiercely competitive economy have grown contemptuous and suspicious of their leaders and their government, regarding them as irrelevant or even destructive. Millions of us apparently see government as uniformly wasteful and inefficient, catering to the unworthy while disrespecting honest hardworking Americans.

By 1994, the accumulated aggravations of twenty years, and disenchantment with liberal Democratic policy in that period, erupted in an outpouring of dissatisfied and irate voters demanding that Democrats be replaced. Voters clearly knew whom they wanted to get rid of but not so clearly what they wanted the replacements to do. On Election Day in 1994, most voters didn't have the slightest idea of the provisions of the Republicans' so-called Contract with America. That notwithstanding, the victors seized the day and since then have seized the headlines with a conservative Republican agenda in both houses fashioned after the Contract's key provisions. Parts of it seem incontestably useful, like procedural reforms and the line-item veto (which the Republicans subsequently and cynically abandoned). But in large part it was designed by distilling the bitterest juices from the people's anger, bottling them as legislation, and then offering it all back as a magic elixir. The result is a concoction that does not deal adequately with either our social or our economic problems.

The Contract espouses a new political philosophy that ignores many of the nation's real needs and real potential, makes negativism an operating principle, and celebrates punishment as the instrument for restoring civility. This New Harshness is a philosophy that takes pleasure in "tough-minded" phrases like "There's no such thing as a free lunch"—and can even justify a certain hard-nosed pride in proposing no lunch at all for some people.

You can hear the New Harshness around us everywhere. A leading Republican senator claims that the social safety net woven during the New Deal and the Great Society has become a "hammock"—thus artfully fostering the image of lazy poor folk lolling about while the rest of America sweats. One wonders if the senator or any of us would really trade places with a typical safety-net beneficiary holding on to that "hammock" for dear life: an elderly woman recovering from a stroke and having some of her medical bills covered by Medicare; an assembly-line worker laid off by downsizing at the factory where he and his dad before him had worked their entire lives; a young mother being sheltered in a home for battered women; a disabled worker receiving Supplemental Security Income (SSI) benefits.

You can see the New Harshness when the Speaker of the House attacks President Clinton as "the enemy of normal Americans"; describes the White House staff as "left-wing elitists"; accuses Democrats of promoting "nihilistic hedonism"; links Woody Allen's personal life and Susan Smith's killing of her two children to policies of the Democratic party; or proclaims that "Crime is not a hard problem. We simply lock up violent criminals until they're too old to be violent. That means fewer welfare workers and more police officers and prosecutors and prisons." Speaker Gingrich seems to have devoted his career to remedying the defect he attributed to his party in a 1978 speech: "One of the great problems in the Republican party is that we don't encourage you to be nasty."

The seeds of the New Harshness are broadcast over the airwaves by a talk-show host who tells his listeners to "kill the sons of bitches"—federal law enforcement agents—with "head shots." Given a chance to retract his remarks in the wake of the bombing of federal offices in Oklahoma City, he merely modified them, suggesting shots to the groin.

Those who speak for the New Harshness rely on crude but effective demagoguery—emotionally laden buzzwords, tried and tested in focus groups. The Republican playbook distributed to GOP candidates before the 1994 elections advised them to identify themselves with "optimistic, positive" words that tested well with samples of voters—words like "liberty," "hard work," "dream," "tough," "opportunity"—and to associate their opponents with words known to generate negative responses, like "bureaucracy," "welfare," "taxes," "waste," and "anti-family."

The problems we face are real. The people's concerns must be addressed. But the apostles of the New Harshness who play so effectively on voters' economic and cultural insecurities do not have the answers we need. When they shift from propaganda to policy their proposals are inadequate and in some cases demonstrably harmful. For the most part, they seek to evade the nation's problems rather than to solve them.

The Republican agenda is not a plan for building a future as much as it is a plan for finding fault. It does not provide the education, infrastructure, research, health care, and international leadership needed to strengthen our economy. Instead, it reduces assistance in all those areas and relies on the discredited magic of supply-side economic theories. It is a politics of shibboleths that will weaken us by fragmentation. It is a plan that offers us catharsis but not a cure.

Outrage is easy, cheap, and oversold. The nation needs less anger and more thoughtful reflection, less shouting and more listening, less dissembling and more honesty. This book tries to look closely at our common problems and proposes a different way of approaching them—together.

In analyzing the issues, we need to remember there is a place for ideology, but it is not first place. First place goes to good sense, no matter what political badge it happens to be wearing at the moment. Sometimes that's common sense . . . other times it may mean uncommon sense. We need to get beyond the beguiling simplistics and sound bites, blow away the blue smoke, take down the political mirrors, and be willing to accept the truth when we find it. For example, some of the solutions will have to inconvenience some Americans, including *us:* sometimes comforting the afflicted does require afflicting the comfortable.

And most of all, to deal effectively with our problems we must understand, accept, and apply one fundamental, indispensable proposition. Without this proposition, nothing else we do will be enough; with it, we can perform real wonders. It is the ancient truth that drove primitive people together to ward off their enemies and wild beasts, to find food and shelter, to raise their children in safety, and eventually to raise up a civilization. Now, in this ever more complex world, we need to accept and apply this basic truth: that we're all in this together, like a family, interconnected and interdependent, and that we cannot afford to revert to a world of "us against them," whether the divide is economic, racial, regional, or philosophical. It is the one great idea that is indispensable to realizing our full potential as a people.

By contrast, in their lust for individualism, the apostles of the New Harshness tempt us with isolation, insularity, and indifference to our opportunities in the wider world and our obligations to one another.

Some of them do it with great glibness and style. The Speaker of the House does it with a flourish, a grin, a cascade of antique historical references that go back four hundred years, and semantic clouds of cyberspace, gigabytes, and nineteen-character passwords for the Internet. But despite all his self-conscious futurism, what he's really offering us is a vision that in many ways would drag us backward to the darkest alleyways of America's first century and egg us on until we agree to dump there in the shadows the weakest parts of our nation, pretending that this triage will somehow make the rest of us stronger.

We've tried that already. It's the way we lived for our first 150 years, for our primitive period when rugged individualism meant dog eat dog unless some private charity provided shelter. When blacks were traded like cattle, women and children were allowed to work for pennies, and men could labor all day, every day for a lifetime and still be poor. When there was no public education or public health care, no workers' compensation or unemployment insurance, no security at the end of life.

America's newest political forces would take us backward, closer to that brutal ethos we first rejected sixty years ago. We should go forward instead, upward together toward the light.

And we can be certain of one thing: the way up is through integration and not disintegration, through synergism not cynicism, through inclusion not exclusion. We must work to build a new sense of community, recognizing that we will achieve our greatest potential as a society not by leaving people by the side of the trail but by moving as many of our people as possible into a new era of productivity and progress—including the struggling workers and the so-called underclass we have come so close to abandoning altogether.

Although some things remain obscure to me after more than two decades in public life, other things are clearer. One is that because the judgments of the electorate control the democratic process, progress depends on the electorate making wiser judgments. The best hope for our democracy lies, as Al Smith observed, in more democracy: the people themselves are the answer.

And that, I hope, is what will make this book useful. If you accept the conventional wisdom, the average voter in America is unabashedly apathetic and misinformed. We all know the old story about the pollster who asked one voter: "Do you believe this country is being hurt by ignorance and apathy?" To which the voter responded: "I don't know, and I don't care."

I don't believe that's where the people are. In my experience, most people want to understand the issues. It's just that the political guides who take it upon themselves to explain things too often have a personal stake in oversimplification and distortion. It's as if you were genuinely interested in learning about automobiles but had only car salesmen to describe the pros and cons of different models. You would be better off with some independent knowledge of cars before stepping inside that showroom, and prospective voters would best serve themselves by acquiring some perspective on the issues before paying too much heed to politicians on the campaign trail.

A British economist once explained that "the purpose of studying economics is not to understand economics; rather it is to avoid being deceived by economists." If this book achieves nothing else, I hope it helps a few voters avoid being deceived by all the different roosters crowing for supremacy in the barnyard of American politics.

There are no magic cures, no simple answers, no road to Utopia. In fact, many of today's hard choices were made necessary by yesterday's attempts at easy answers. But if we examine the facts and guard against irrelevance and distortion, we can make real progress, so that ten and twenty and fifty years from now, our country will be even stronger, more united, more prosperous, and more just than it is today. This book is intended to help move us vigorously and securely in that direction by describing the kinds of attitudes and actions we need to move forward instead of backward.

And it occurs to me that it may even be unique in at least one respect. It just may be the only book in print on America's social and political situation that neither quotes, cites, nor purports to paraphrase Alexis de Tocqueville. It will from time to time, however, tip its hat to Momma.

This spring, after a long illness that led her away from us gradually over several years, my family and I lost the extraordinary heart and soul that was my mother. Frankly, I have always felt her immortality was assured—not only theologically, but because she lives on in so many of us who knew her as a permanent spring of earthy, earthly, tough, tart, implacable, astonishing wisdom.

An uneducated immigrant woman who never felt comfortable with English, who grew up on a remote farm in Italy without electricity or running water, she was the truest sounding board I ever found, whether the issue was the discipline of one of her grandchildren or the direction of grand public policy. If, in my stumbling Italian, I couldn't explain a decision to Momma, it was probably a bad idea. And she always cut to the heart of the matter: "How come you're governor, but everybody still has to wait two hours for a driver's license?"

Like my father, Andrea, Immaculata Cuomo didn't spend much time imparting abstract lessons of the world, but, through the simple example of her life—her absolute devotion to family and her sharply unsentimental struggle to make a place for us in

America—she taught us all perhaps the most important lesson: that what is right is usually also what is necessary; that in helping one another we almost always help ourselves.

In the end, this book is simply a tribute to her good sense— and to all that she proved was possible in America.

2

The Dream Deferred

—

In today's sour atmosphere, it's easy to forget how extraordinary this country is, but we remain by many measures the greatest nation in history.

From the Bill of Rights onward we have been an international beacon of basic human freedoms and liberties, advocating the belief that all people should have equal rights, and while we have often fallen short of that ideal, we have been impelled continually toward it. We are still the freest society on earth, and share the benefits of the biggest, broadest, most robust and durable democracy ever created, an inspirational example that has helped bring down totalitarianism and communism around the world.

Our visions of equality, liberty, and justice, expressed in the Declaration of Independence, the Bill of Rights, and the Preamble to the Constitution, greatly influence the structure of our political system and the course of our conduct. They are like a dream that we consciously strive to make real. As historian James Truslow Adams put it sixty-four years ago:

The American Dream . . . has not been a dream of merely material plenty, though that has doubtless counted heavily. It has been much more than that. It has been a dream of being able to grow to fullest development as man and woman, unhampered by the barriers which had slowly been erected in older civilizations, unrepressed by social orders which had developed for the benefit of classes rather than for the simple human being of any and every class. And that dream has been realized more fully in actual life here than anywhere else, though very imperfectly. . . .

In our second century as a nation, we began to learn to pool our resources, through government, to cushion ourselves against the unavoidable perils of the free market. With unemployment insurance, workers' compensation, Social Security, fair labor standards, Aid to Families with Dependent Children (AFDC), Medicare, and Medicaid, we improved our living standards and working conditions, provided services that benefit and strengthen us, and protected and nurtured our most vulnerable members. In doing so, we amplified our potential for greatness.

And despite its ups and downs, our economy has helped generate tremendous wealth for individuals—we lead the world in millionaires and billionaires—and it has produced a decent standard of living for millions, the children of seekers, many of whom came from parts of the world where they had little reason to hope for anything but lifelong deprivation.

Then why are we so unhappy?

The truth is, we are struggling with several kinds of disappointment. After decades of rising expectations, we are disillusioned by our current economic prospects. The American Dream has grown elusive. Despite a reasonably strong economy, low or moderately skilled workers are being laid off or left behind. We are also frustrated by America's inability to reverse social crises we once imagined we could erase altogether. Our social programs have improved things but not enough. And perhaps most of all, we are irritated by the inability of political leaders of both major parties to help us out of these predicaments.

Most of that irritation recently, however, has been directed against the Democrats, and not entirely without cause. Although Democrats from Franklin D. Roosevelt on could properly claim that they helped millions realize the aspirations of the American Dream, some of our excesses and omissions have contributed to the nation's current disenchantment.

To some extent, the errors of the Democrats have been "too much of a good thing"—good ideas and beneficent instincts carried a little too far.

I say that lovingly as a lifelong Democrat who found the faith much the same way I became a Catholic—baptized, before I was old enough to question it—by the deep current of Democratic loyalty that ran through our old working-class immigrant neighborhood. I have kept the faith all these years because the party has always offered a brand of aspiration I found impossible to resist, a sense that we could make ourselves better, as individuals and as a society, and that there was more to life than waging the war for maximum personal luxury.

But that high-mindedness is where the trouble started.

Idealism has its own vices, and our party, at one time or another, has indulged in most of them, from simple self-righteousness and rigid dogmatism to a willful refusal to face facts. Knowing how badly the poor, the elderly, the disadvantaged needed us, and feeling a little too sure we and they were on God's side of every issue, we slighted the steady middle-class gal who "brung us to the dance." In striving to help all those least able to help themselves—the victims of discrimination and oppression, those without power or property—we have too often neglected the concerns of the "working stiff," blue-, pink-, or white-collar, of every skin color, who labors hard and lives modestly—the Andrea and Immaculata Cuomos everywhere. And perhaps most important, we have failed to show both the poor and those in the middle how much all our interests coincide. We should have found more compelling ways to explain how, when we invest in things like public education, good nutrition, drug abuse prevention, pollution control, medical research, or even midnight basketball, we all benefit, whether or not the programs serve us directly.

In those instances where interests collide, the flash points where those who have a little feel threatened by those who have less, we Democrats have not worked hard enough at finding ways to harmonize the competing interests. All too often we have let the political process respond to the loudest scream. At the same time, we have appeared sometimes to be squeamish about punishment of any kind. Even as we advocated the wisdom and efficiency of dealing with root causes and struggled to make our justice system fairer and more humane, we should have been clearer in recognizing the indispensability of deterrence through law enforcement and vigorous sentencing. While correctly recognizing the social and economic conditions that provide fertile ground for the weeds of crime and other social pathologies, we have too often given the impression that we sought to "understand" rather than condemn antisocial and criminal behavior.

And we should have made clearer our commitment to basic values like the dignity of hard work, responsibility for the children you bring into this world and the parents who brought you, respect for family and reverence for country.

Understanding all the good things that government has achieved in our lifetimes, Democrats have not been aggressive enough in guarding against its failures. If a government program was born from good intentions, we have tended to defend it against criticism or reform, even if the evidence suggested plainly the program was not working as it should. Beyond the obvious fact that preserving ineffective programs helps no one, the truth is that by being advocates for government activism without being zealots for government efficiency, we left the door wide open for Republicans to cite any and every imperfect program as proof that government can't do anything right—and shouldn't even try.

It seems to me that we've been making these mistakes for at least the last two decades. In my first political speech, addressing the New Democratic Coalition in 1974, I said:

This is the real challenge for our party . . . to serve the poor without crushing the middle class. And while doing this . . . to make clear to the middle class that it isn't our intention to crush them.

It can be done . . . if we have the humility and decency to remember that all the angels seldom stand on one side of a particular issue. And that in the subtle conflict situations, not every resistance to what seems a good idea is bigotry, and not every new liberal idea is infallible.

If we can have the restraint not to torment the middle class with arrogant and insensitive rhetoric, nor to patronize the poor with artificial and academic sociological propositions to which they themselves attach no real value. . . . It can be done. More importantly, it must be done, and it must be done by us. Because the alternative is not only to lose the election, but to leave these dangerous problems to the callousness of a Republican party that thrives on polarizing people, that exploits fear and hate. A Republican party that will seduce the middle class by pandering to its worst instincts in these dangerous situations and then, with the heavy hammer forged out of the coalition of rich and middle class, will beat the poor into even greater submission.

None of these errors has been true of all Democrats, but enough of us have been guilty of these omissions often enough that our party has paid the price in lost respect and loyalty. Now —as some of us anticipated twenty years ago—the Republicans and conservatives together have seized the day, sowing a harsh new crop of politics in the deep soil of our disappointments and disillusionments.

Having admitted the mistakes of the past, however, we should also keep in mind our successes, not only as Democrats but as Americans as well. At times like this, when we are so prone to be skeptical about our government and so tempted to doubt whether our efforts to reason and work together can yield positive change, it helps to have a good memory. Just in my lifetime, the progress we have achieved—and grown accustomed to— more than justifies a faith in our ability to work collectively to move ahead to a higher plane of civility and strength.

I remember an America when women were still getting used to the idea that they could vote; when a man who hit his wife was a lout but within his rights; when most women had at best only three careers open to them besides motherhood: secretary, teacher, or nurse. Today, the women's vote is a factor in many political races—and women candidates are players in many more; domestic violence is acknowledged as both a crime and a crisis; and our law schools and medical schools are enrolling women in record numbers.

I remember an America before civil rights laws, when bigotry was casual, ruthless, and legitimized by countless laws and many of our most prestigious institutions; when Marian Anderson wasn't allowed to sing at Constitution Hall because she was black; when no black players were allowed in the major leagues —and Jackie Robinson faced boos and worse every time he strode to the plate. We have a long way to go before we wash ourselves clean of the stain of racial prejudice, but at least we have come to know it when we see it, to call it by its right name, and to make laws to prevent it. Americans of color make up a disproportionately large percentage of our disadvantaged population, but in increasing numbers they are rising to the highest ranks in practically every hierarchy of talent in America, and with the doors these pioneers have broken open, the momentum is building for greater change.

My parents lived in an America before Social Security, before food stamps, before Medicare—where a widow on the block would simply go hungry if my parents didn't feed her with scraps from their small grocery store. An America in which children would sometimes stay home from school because they couldn't go barefoot and there wasn't the money for a pair of shoes. An America in which, less than three decades ago, Bobby Kennedy brought us face-to-face with what Michael Harrington had termed "The Other America," the one that included "children in the Delta area of Mississippi with distended stomachs, whose faces [were] covered with sores from starvation." An America most of us find hard to imagine now.

I remember an America where a man could come home from

a factory missing three fingers and the best compensation he could hope for was a basket of fruit from the company at Christmas; where factories towered over residential neighborhoods and nobody asked what was coming out of the smokestack; where raw sewage was the only kind there was.

All these dismal things belong to history now—to the early period before we decided it was good to come together to help one another—and all of them were rooted out by the sharp spade of our democratic government. To say that the New Deal, the Great Society, and all the other progressive initiatives of federal and state government in the last sixty years have failed to make us perfect would be accurate. To say they failed to improve upon the wretched social catastrophes created by the 150 years of macho individualism that preceded them would be foolish indeed.

We are, however, still a young nation, vigorous yet imperfect. We're like a sixteen-year-old boy with big muscles, a natural swing, and a great career ahead of us—but we've mistaken a hot streak at the plate for a guarantee of playing winning ball season after season.

If we want to stay at the top in a league that's getting tougher all the time, we have a lot of work to do. And as any coach will tell you, you can't get better until you know what you're doing wrong.

We have to look back a bit to find that out.

I have lived through the entire era since the great change came in the 1930s. I stepped into the hopeful years after high school just at the moment that America was dusting herself off from World War II—the last "good" war we ever fought. The fact that the Good Guys came so close to losing only made victory sweeter in the end.

After our triumph, we knew who we were: a tough, bright, just, bighearted people who could beat up anyone on the block but didn't want to; we wanted to build a great nation instead. We knew where we were going and we couldn't be stopped.

But that's not what the economists predicted. They told us, "Congratulations, you won World War II. Now think back to what happened right before the war. Remember a black ditch called the Great Depression that was a dozen years deep? When you get all those GIs shipped home, they'll find the defense industry shut down, markets overseas destroyed, our women back in the kitchens, and our economy back in a rut. There'll be bread lines and massive unemployment all over again." We proved the economists wrong. Instead of faltering, we lit the fuse on a quarter-century of the most explosive economic growth in our history—fireworks that went on so long we thought they would last forever.

The Baby Boom helped. So did our natural resources. All our obvious competitors, friend and foe, had been virtually leveled by the war, while our own infrastructure and factories, and the great majority of our people, were still intact, raring to work in our vigorous free enterprise economy.

Despite these advantages, the private sector alone couldn't do all that needed doing. Much of our success was shaped or sparked by the actions of our government. The GI Bill helped hundreds of thousands of Americans go to college or trade schools, preparing them to work in a host of industries that sprang from new technologies developed during the war. And the colossal ambition of the interstate highway system that President Eisenhower conceived to tie us all together created work for hundreds of thousands of Americans. By helping both Japan and Europe to get back on their feet through massive infusions of manpower, materials, and finances, we used our government to rebuild markets that were ravenous for our goods.

Putting all of this private strength and government support together, we became the world's master builders, sellers, creditors, and bankers. We made the things that everybody wanted: cars, TVs, tools, toasters, clothes—and the marks, yen, and lire kept pouring in the door. On the gates of the Bethlehem Steel plant, near Buffalo, New York, the "Help Wanted" sign was a permanent fixture. There was work for everybody and good pay, enough to buy all you needed for the American Dream—a house, a car, a new refrigerator, a new TV, a good vacation, and tickets to see Mays, Mantle, and Snider, all in the same year. And all with just one salary in the family. Wow . . . the American Dream indeed!

The economy kept right on blooming, sending out new shoots and branches right up to the early 1970s without much regard to the stormy social and political forces raging overhead: the poisonous rain of McCarthyism; the long, hot summer of the battle for civil rights; the stirring breezes of the fight for women's liberation and for release from every kind of stultifying convention; the terrible thunderhead of Vietnam; the climatic shift that came when hard drugs infiltrated the cities and all the attendant crime and violence took over the streets. And then, the bleak winter of Watergate.

The country was changing fast, and not all for the better. Perhaps we became spoiled by success during this period of American hegemony. Children born into affluence began to lose some of the drive and ambition of their parents, who had immigrated here or been born during the Depression. Our giant corporations took their markets for granted. Our powerful unions took their jobs for granted and workers began to take their unions for granted, as all of us became accustomed to the basic rights and living standards the unions had gained for workers.

A new, eager, freer explorative culture arose that inspired some positive things like greater environmental awareness, but also spawned many excesses rooted in disrespect for authority and for hard work. "Do your own thing" became the password and the standard for a lot of young people and even for some adults who used to "Do it by the book." An advertising-driven consumer culture exalted immediate gratification above the traditional virtues of discipline and self-restraint, and the media projected it all—along with a sick fascination with violence—everywhere in stereo and three dimensions. Bored kids in the suburbs, excited to a new pitch, started to fool around with drugs.

A number of terrible episodes traumatized us spiritually. We lost three heroes to madmen. We lost a President to ignominy. We lost a war to hubris. In the space of twenty years, we lost much of our reassurance and our inspiration and we couldn't find anything to take their place. We had no great unifying cause —World War II was the last—no orthodoxies, no heroes. We couldn't figure out what to do about the hole in our hearts. Paul

Simon gave us the plaintive cry of the times: "Where have you gone, Joe DiMaggio? A nation turns its lonely eyes to you."

In the meantime, while we weren't looking, much of the rest of the world outside the Soviet Union was getting hungrier and stronger, the way we had been during and just after World War II. By the late 1970s, Germany and Japan were economic power-houses and the oil-producing nations were flexing their might. They had become vigorous while we were testing out the arm-chair of prosperity that had come to seem like an American birthright. In the 1950s, "Made in Japan" meant it would break if you dropped it. By the mid-1970s, "Made in Japan" meant when you closed a door on one of their cars, it sounded like the door on a bank vault. We started buying their cars instead of our own. We started losing jobs and markets, not only to the Japanese but also to other nations whose workers were delighted with a frac-tion of our wages, and couldn't imagine, much less demand, the pensions and health insurance and vacation time we took for granted.

From 1945 to 1970, we had been the makers, the sellers, the greatest creditors in the world. Beginning in the early 1970s, we began the slide that would leave us buyers and borrowers and the biggest debtor nation on earth. Today, we send billions of dollars to Germany, Japan, and other nations to buy from them goods that we used to make and sell to them. Then we borrow back the dollars, paying billions more in interest.

Most Americans didn't recognize all of this while it was first happening. The recession of 1982 was sobering, but for most of the 1980s we worked hard on believing that our economy could make gold out of junk. Socially, the catastrophes multiplied and became more horribly evident. Before 1982, no one had ever heard of AIDS or crack or the homeless; by 1984, they were dominant facts in the life of every American city. Young girls were having babies before they had learned to work, let alone to parent, and in surroundings that offered neither them nor their children any real hope. Each new drug that hit the streets produced a new round of addicts—and brutal new wars over turf. The crime that had been escalating for years, magnified by an almost voyeuristic obsession with blood and chaos on the television news, finally began to seem intolerable. We won the Cold War, yet we didn't feel like winners.

In the early 1990s, recession struck again—the worst economic downturn since the 1930s—and the ensuing recovery has been slow and anything but evenhanded. Computerization and globalization continue at a dizzying clip, threatening to displace millions of workers.

This sad and frightening decline has left many Americans angry and frustrated. Economic insecurities and a simultaneous sense that we're drifting from our cultural moorings have tempted many of us to lash out at scapegoats and to oust whoever's in power. The voters knocked the Republicans out of the White House in 1992. Just two years later, they turned against the Democrats. And now we approach another major election.

Some of us try to console ourselves with the hopeful prayer that some third-party savior will rescue us, but we have no clear idea of what such a savior would do or say. In all likelihood, we will settle on a candidate from one of the two familiar parties. No matter whom we turn to for answers, however, we should demand that they help us tackle the real threats to our country —rather than merely using our anxiety and anger to help tackle their political opponents. We should make them tell us what they intend to do about the two major problems that block our path toward a higher ground, problems that, like fraternal twins, are distinguishable but profoundly interconnected: our complex economic predicament and our devastating cultural corrosion.

America's Twin Challenges

The Economy: Falling Behind on the Treadmill

Flip through the business section of any newspaper and think how often you see startling pairs of headlines like these: "Record Earnings. Layoffs Announced." We could understand headlines that said, "Earnings Off. Layoffs Announced." But why should there be layoffs if the company is doing so well?

We are living with a tormenting new problem: an economy that is rewarding investors amply but is not providing good-paying jobs for average workers. The stock market is up, but wages are down. Those at the top of the economic ladder are enjoying the view; those in the middle find the next rung up harder to reach; those at the bottom are in danger of falling off altogether.

Since the late 1970s, most American workers have experienced a drop in their real hourly pay. For individual families, it means that today there's less buying power in each paycheck than there used to be—significantly less. Blue-collar workers and those with less than a college degree suffered the steepest wage drops. Since 1989, however, even white-collar, college-educated workers have lost ground, as corporate "restructurings" discarded unprecedented numbers of middle-management employees.

During most of the 1980s, families were doing better, even as hourly wages declined, but only because they worked harder to make ends meet. There were more households in which both husband and wife worked full-time, or even juggled more than one job each. They may have been frazzled and had less time to devote to their children and their local PTA, but by working longer hours these two-earner households temporarily held on to their place on the economic ladder.

Since 1989, the picture has become bleaker. Family income dropped by 7 percent in just four years. As you would expect, it fell during the recession of 1990 and 1991, but it kept falling during the so-called recovery of 1992 and 1993 as well. By 1993, in fact, family income had actually fallen back below its 1979 level.

Some of us have been sliding backward. And it doesn't look as though the slide is going to stop despite some economic assumptions we used to depend on. Economists have traditionally agreed that increased productivity is the road to greater prosperity. The more we produced, the larger the pie—and that meant larger slices for everybody. But the latest data show that even though the pie is growing all the time, the slices for a lot of average workers keep getting smaller.

There goes the American Dream! Only a handful of today's young graduates can even imagine having a family, a house, a car, a new refrigerator, a TV, a vacation, and tickets to see Michael Jordan, all on a single salary.

For decades, the American Dream was built on the assumption that the income our economy generated was becoming more evenly distributed. Henry Ford taught us by unforgettable example that business prospers if workers are paid sufficiently to afford to buy the things they build. The labor unions, fighting for a decent day's pay for a hard day's work, helped not only their members but our entire economy; if the steel industry prospered, steel executives got raises, but so did foundry workers. Our middle class was no slim cushion of shopkeepers buffering the rich from the poor. Our middle class—big, prosperous, and growing—was America itself!

That's the way it used to be.

Now, income inequality is widening. Put simply, executives and professionals are earning a larger share of the pie, and everybody else is getting a smaller one.

This growing skew in incomes would be bad enough, but it's compounded by an even more dramatic imbalance in wealth. If income is how much money you earn in a given year, wealth is the value of the assets you own. For most people, that's primarily a home and a small bank account. For those fortunate enough to have money to invest, it also includes stocks and bonds.

Money breeds money, of course. If you own $1 million in bonds that pay 5 percent interest, you can earn $50,000 per year in interest alone—far more than most Americans earn by working forty hours a week, fifty weeks a year. If a corporation slashes wages or benefits to employees or lays them off, the workers' income will drop but, quite often, the company's profits will rise, and so will its stock and thus the wealth of its shareholders.

That's one reason why wealth in this country has grown even more unequal than income. By 1989, the top 20 percent of households controlled 85 percent of the country's wealth. The

remaining 80 percent of the people shared what was left: a mere
15 percent. A free enterprise system is bound to produce inequality of wealth. That's a price we pay for unlimited personal
opportunity, and no doubt Americans are willing to pay it. But
how much inequality is reasonable? Is it right that America now
has the most unequal distribution of wealth among all industrial
nations, including Great Britain, Canada, Italy, France, and Germany?

At the bottom of the economic ladder, poverty remains intrac-
table—even in recent periods of overall economic growth. The
rising tide, it seems, no longer lifts the rowboats. By 1993, nearly
one out of six Americans was poor. That's over 39 million Americans living in poverty, 7 million more poor than in 1989. Tragically, the younger you are, the more likely you are to be poor.
More than one in five children under eighteen lives in poverty,
as does more than one in four children under six. Among young
black children, over half are poor. Shockingly, despite America's
great affluence, poor children in our country are actually worse
off than poor children in nearly every other Western industrialized nation, and the gap between our poorest and richest children is the widest.

We now have three categories of workers: those with full-
time, well-paid positions with adequate benefits; those with part-
time, temporary, or low-paying jobs without benefits; and the
unemployed, some with such dim prospects of finding work that
they have given up looking altogether.

For millions stuck in low-paying jobs, work does not provide
economic security or dignity or the opportunity to advance. The
larger part of working Americans, those not lucky enough to
have the kind of education or training that meets industry's needs
today, are frightened by prospects of continuing low wages,
fewer benefits, reduction in hours of work, or, worst of all, layoffs. Some corporations are treating their workers as disposable
commodities, just cogs of production to be acquired at the lowest
possible cost rather than as long-term assets to be nurtured. It's
like the apocryphal story about the company that ran a contest
to solicit money-saving ideas from employees, promising any
worker whose suggestion was used a prize equal to 25 percent

of the money it saved. After reviewing the entries, the company gave only one prize; it went to an employee who suggested the award be cut to 10 percent! It has to be tough to throw yourself into your work if your bosses see you as nothing better than a necessary evil.

Indeed, there is some evidence that the entire downsizing syndrome may have passed the point of diminishing returns, producing what has been called "corporate anorexia." In some places, the cutting has become so extreme that companies have been left undernourished and unable to grow, with employees stretched to the limit and morale at a dangerous low. For many businesses, not growing inevitably means fading away. That's a good lesson, not just for austerity-conscious business but for the nation as a whole: we must invest in our people in order to grow.

No one begrudges the successful their success. That's the free enterprise system. That's the American Dream! Certainly that's what my parents believed. One day, at the governor's mansion, my mother saw Lee Iacocca's picture on a magazine cover and, unable to read the headline but suspecting he was Italian, she asked me about him. I told her it was a story about the millions of dollars he earns every year. She said, "What does he do?" I said, "He's the boss at Chrysler; they make cars." She said, "What's the matter, you don't know how to make a car?"

I'm sure my mother thought of Lee Iacocca as being a much bigger success than her son the governor. I'm sure Lee's mother did, too. Lee says, "America was the land of freedom, the freedom to become anything you wanted to be, if you wanted it bad enough and were willing to work for it." That's good. But if only the rich are getting richer while the poor are getting poorer and those in the middle are slipping backward, something is amiss. If only those who own the grindstones prosper, while those who keep their noses to the grindstones have nothing to show for it but bruised noses, the glorious machinery of the American economy is out of whack.

No wonder millions of voters are restless, dissatisfied, frustrated, angry, and just plain worried. No wonder 85 percent of Americans now believe that the American Dream will be harder to achieve in the future than it used to be.

• • •

Some parts of our economic trouble are tangible, as personal and obvious as your brother-in-law moving into your living room after he gets laid off. But there's another, more abstract piece of the puzzle that in its long-term effects may actually be worse.

The typical American family is finding it harder and harder to make ends meet, to make sure there's enough money in the checking account to pay each month's bills. Saving for college or retirement or even a rainy day seems close to impossible.

And the startling fact is that the family of America is in about the same fix, or worse. As a nation, we—the federal government—are spending too much, and borrowing too much, and not saving or investing enough. Yet although politicians seem to drone and rant about these dire abstractions all the time, most Americans have a hard time summoning up any sense of urgency about them. "Debt, deficit—what's the difference? And what's the big deal? The government never actually shuts down."

What is the deficit? Currently, the federal government spends about $200 billion more each year than it takes in. A little context: during the years Jimmy Carter was President, the annual deficit ranged between $40 billion and $79 billion. During the 1960s, the deficit rose above $10 billion only once!

Without dramatic changes in the way we spend and the way we produce revenues, the deficit is projected to continue at high levels. By the turn of the century, it will approach $300 billion, and if present spending and revenue patterns continue, it will soar to $400 billion ten years from now. And it's not as if all this deficit spending is being added to a clean slate. It's one thing to start off in the black and then run up charges on your credit card. It's another thing to keep running up new credit card charges when you've already amassed a hefty balance you're not equipped to pay.

The federal government—which means *us*—has already accumulated nearly $5 trillion in debt. That's trillion, with a "tr," as in trouble. Each year, that debt leaps upward, by exactly the amount of the annual *deficit*. Between 1996 and 2000, the national debt will swell by another $1.5 trillion.

Some of that debt the government "owes to itself"—for example, every year the Social Security trust fund lends billions to the government's general funds. But even if you subtract the portion of federal debt owed to government accounts, the debt is staggering. In 1992, for the first time, the federal debt owed to the public, that is, to outside investors, was more than half the entire gross domestic product (GDP). The debt as a percentage of GDP is projected to rise each and every year, inexorably, unless we do something more about it.

There are many negative consequences of such massive debt. Some of them are long-term but at least one is immediate, affecting your take-home pay and the quality of the services you receive from your government. Each year, well over $200 billion of our tax dollars goes to pay the interest on the national debt. That's equivalent to more than one out of every three income tax dollars withheld from your paycheck. Looked at another way, it's more than the federal government spends on education and job training, highways and aviation, environmental and energy programs, and criminal justice—put together. To put it in business terms, the opportunity cost is unconscionable: imagine all the good we could do with that money if it weren't being shoveled out to cover the interest on our accumulated failure to pay for what we've spent.

And there is another deficit confronting government: an investment deficit, the shortfall between the public investments we need and our actual expenditures. Investment is money spent on something that will be used to produce or maintain wealth. Public sector investments include highways, bridges, water systems, pollution controls, and airports—physical facilities, commonly referred to as infrastructure: the underlying foundations of our economy. They also include outlays for education and training—investments in people, what economists like to call human capital, that develop a more skilled and productive workforce. And they include investments in scientific research to improve our standard of living and enhance our quality of life.

It's not hard to understand how these investments pay off. It's a bit like the old saying "Give a man a fish and you feed him for a day. Teach a man to fish and he can feed himself forever."

Buying a platter of fish to eat is not an investment; it enables you to consume a tasty meal, but nothing more. Teaching your children the skill of fishing—now, that's an investment, because it will result in more fish tomorrow. Acquiring a boat and fishing gear—that's an investment in physical assets that will also help bring in more fish. Conducting research in marine biology and aquaculture—you can see how in the long run that, too, is an investment that can yield more fish.

Federal outlays for investments, other than defense-related investments, were cut drastically during the early 1980s under President Reagan. In inflation-adjusted terms, civilian research and development was cut 30 percent, education and training 25 percent, and physical infrastructure 13 percent. Even with some modest growth in recent years, total nondefense federal investment in the 1990s constitutes a smaller share of our total economy—less than 2 percent of the gross domestic product—than it did during the 1960s and 1970s. The United States ranks fourteenth out of sixteen industrialized nations in expenditures for elementary and secondary schooling—and we have the embarrassing test scores to prove it. We rank far below nations like Japan, France, and Germany in net investment in infrastructure. As a result, many of our public facilities and institutions are outdated, inadequate, or poorly maintained, requiring major rehabilitation or replacement. Like potholes slowing traffic, our lack of investment in public infrastructure has slowed the pace of economic growth.

In short, government is spending beyond its means—and yet it is not investing wisely in the very things that would bolster our economy in the long run.

Cultural Corrosion

At the same time the great engine of our economy sputters, there is around us evidence of a new and nearly inexplicable cultural corrosion manifest in everything from drugs, violence, and teen pregnancy to a growing incivility, crudity, and alienation. We are surely a long way from Momma's mountainside in Salerno, or

even from the poor but hopeful streets of the Queens neighborhood I grew up in. In my generation, all of us, no matter what
our political philosophy, feel that distance, and we feel it as a
pain. In honest moments we feel it as a shame, too.

Surely, many things were terrible in "the good old days."
Human beings have been prone to brutality and bad judgment
for a thousand centuries, but nothing can explain away the data
that describe our current predicament.

Think about it: the rate of births among unmarried teenagers
nearly tripled over the past three decades. Each year, about one
million teenage girls get pregnant.

Today, close to one-third of all children are born out of
wedlock.

In 1960, less than 10 percent of families with children were
headed by a single parent. Now, 30 percent are. These single-
parent households, mostly headed by women, are six times more
likely to be poor than married-couple families. Many of these
result from divorce. But increasingly, there was no marriage at
any time.

Although the overall number of drug users is lower than the
peak rate of the late 1970s, there are between 1.5 and 2.5 million
users of cocaine and crack. Since 1990, as the potency of street
drugs has increased, drug-related emergency room visits have
been rising. Heroin has begun making a frightful comeback
among the jaded younger generation.

The Justice Department estimates that eight out of ten Americans can expect to be a victim of violent crime at least once in
their lives.

Particularly horrifying is the fact that the face of the criminal
is increasingly a child's face: children are the fastest growing
segment of the total criminal population, and juvenile arrests for
violent crimes, including murder, are surging. At the same time,
teenagers are two and a half times more likely to be the victims
of violent crime than adults.

The apparent breakdown of moral standards is both reflected
in the media and to some degree influenced by that media—
from the traditional sources like radio, TV, movies, and popular

music as well as the new wave of purveyors: video games, CD-ROM, and even on-line bulletin boards.

Psychologists have demonstrated that overexposure to violent programming has damaging effects on children. So—does the fact that the average child views a cumulative total of up to 8,000 murders and 100,000 acts of violence on television sound like overexposure to you?

Fifty-six percent of Americans believe that television has the greatest single influence on children's values—more than parents, teachers, or religious leaders combined. So, should it bother us that when *USA Today* monitored a week of prime-time network TV only four of the forty-five sex scenes involved couples who were married? Yes, I think so. When the average teenager spends twenty-one hours a week watching television, compared to about five hours doing homework, less than two hours reading, and less than three hours a week alone with either parent, it is past time to worry and about time to do something.

Also troubling is a general harshness in American life that seeps through our politics, sours our daily experiences, and sometimes even jeopardizes our lives.

It is sickeningly clear in our enthusiasm for "tough" new solutions: "No welfare! No milk money! No school lunches! We don't want to pay for 'those people'—and besides, it's their own fault!" Or the fact that in 1995, the line that drew the loudest and most sustained applause in the inaugural speech of New York Governor George Pataki was his promise to bring back the death penalty as fast as he possibly could.

The harshness is evident in the popularity of hate radio, where diatribe replaces dialogue, the hosts and listeners feed off each other's bile, and the ratings jump off the charts because millions of us love it.

It is even manifest in the alarming increase in traffic deaths, which police and transportation officials attribute to more aggressive motorists. Says the state superintendent of police in Maryland, where traffic deaths rose 28 percent in just one year: "There is an attitude on the roadway that is reflecting a general attitude that we're seeing in society today." Observes a former federal highway administrator: "It looks like everyone on the road is coming out with two purposes in mind. You've got your overriding trip purpose of getting where you're going and the purpose of never giving an inch to the next guy." Doesn't that sum up not only many private attitudes but also much of what passes for political thinking in today's climate? "Never give an inch to the next guy" as you make your way through the world.

Unfortunately, the coarse scales of our harsh attitudes toward one another conceal something else just as unattractive and disturbing: an underbelly of self-indulgence, particularly the loss of a compelling sense of individual responsibility—to pull your own weight, save for the future, put your children's needs before your own, or give something back to the community.

And perhaps one thing worries us more than all the rest: the creeping sense that we are losing the old values that made life worth living and more civilized than it is now. We are beginning to sense that there's something profound at work here. A disorienting loss of faith in some larger, transcendent, binding truth to believe in, to follow, to hold on to against the tide.

Most Americans acknowledge these problems and are concerned by them; people of my generation and my age, who can remember when times were different, are particularly unnerved even though we will not bear the full brunt of the consequences. Coming of age in the early 1950s, we were able to afford a house, to raise a family, to earn a decent living, to live our lives guided by solid values, and to count on Social Security benefits to cushion our retirement. It's the younger generation, and their children to come, that we worry about the most: will they have these same comforts, or will the good life, both materially and spiritually, be beyond their reach?

Certainly, much of our current predicament seems inexplicable, even to those of us who make a study of it. But whether we can explain it all or not, we can sense it, and appreciate its severity. By any measure, America's social well-being is at a dangerously low point, and it's not improving.

From our economy to our culture, we are facing problems that are big, awkward, expensive, even repugnant. They will never get better on their own. They will never get better if we pretend they don't exist or insist that they're not our responsibility. And they will never quiet down if we just shout at them to shut up.

But that's just about all the New Harshness does, as the next chapter will demonstrate.

3

Running Hard
Backward:
The Contract
with America

—

Today's radical Republicans appear to have borrowed an insight from a different time and a different kind of radical, although one with a notably similar hostility to government. It was Jerry Rubin, a hippie counterculture leader from the 1960s, who observed that "the power to define the situation is the ultimate power." That's precisely the power the Republicans have flaunted since they seized the national microphone in November 1994 and made the rest of us listen. And listen and listen.

Maybe the reason they sound so insistent and so loud is that the only other voices we've heard have been too faint and too fragmented. Up from the aisles occupied by Democrats wafts a fitful stream of grumbles and objections, but so far they have been no match for the Republican leaders, whose firm grasp of the podium is matched by the loud applause of their supporters in the audience. Without stronger and more persuasive voices raised in opposition, the incessant stream of glib and appealing shibboleths and generalities looks tempting to a lot of Americans. The Republicans seem to have their act together so well, you have to wonder: if the new Speaker and his followers are in fact as wrong as they seem to be, how come so many people seem to think they're right? Maybe it's true that what's sapping the strength of this mighty nation is a plague of teenage girls and their babies luxuriating in tenements and trailer parks from coast to coast—while being gradually corrupted by Bill Moyers and his liberal accomplices on public TV. Maybe Reagan-style supply-side economics would really work this time and its crushing legacy of debt is just an inconvenient coincidence. Maybe it's true that all the vice in politics spews forth from Washington, and all the virtue bubbles up from the pure spring of the states, and that local governments will divide their cornucopia of block grants with such exquisite fairness and intelligence that the federal government can just stick to raising armies and exploring outer space. Maybe it's true that all we really need to renew American civilization is an Uzi in every pot.

I don't think so . . . and gradually more people are coming to that view. Things are changing. Gradually, as America tries to wrap the Contract's soaring general propositions around the awkward shape of our reality, its gaps and flaws have begun to show. It's already clear that with respect to our most serious social and economic problems, the Contract with America offers us a dose of evasion, distraction, and half-measures that won't help us get any better and will actually make some of our problems worse. Most of its errors proceed from a failure to see that we Americans are not 250 million lone cowboys, each galloping toward our own individual sunset, but rather fellow passengers sharing a lifelong ride on the same extraordinary train.

If I were limited to just one criticism of the Contract, it would be this: it demands no more of our political leaders than that they set sail in whatever direction the political winds seem to be blowing—as measured by the cheap tin weathervane of the latest opinion polls. Despite its bold rhetoric, the Contract essentially abdicates any responsibility for genuine political foresight, analysis, or leadership, offering us instead the top ten popular complaints and top ten appealing home remedies. But even taken all together, they don't begin to solve the major problems we face today.

By promoting tax cuts for the middle class and the wealthy, and singing the praises of supply-side economics, the Contract tells us things we find easy to believe, saying, in effect, "The government is wasteful, so we can solve our fiscal problems painlessly by just taking some of our money back—and nobody gets hurt." By making welfare reform and immigration central issues, it gives us someone easy to blame, although by no fair measure can either of these legitimate concerns be regarded as principal causes of our fiscal or social problems. By exploiting popular misconceptions about the percentage of the budget we spend on foreign aid, it leads us to believe that isolationism would produce a windfall. By playing up the death penalty and punishment in general, the Contract avoids the more difficult truth that all the punishment in the world would not be enough to correct what's gone wrong with this country and that we will have to invest in our future if we want to reap dividends.

Generally, by castigating all those involved in the social deterioration, the Contract gives us a catharsis. It lets us stamp our feet and wave banners for all-American propositions—like "the free market" and "the thousand points of light"—while telling us that the facts and details get confusing, so we should just comfort ourselves with easy simplistics instead.

We can all applaud the slogans. Do we believe in the virtues of the free market? Of course. Our entire way of life depends on the strength and vitality of America's companies, from the industrial giants to the one-person start-ups. But every one of us knows that "free enterprise" is not a perfect system that guarantees, without some help from government, all the jobs and economic strength we need. We'd have no Chrysler if the market were totally free of government influence. Should we have abandoned the savings and loans, even though they were victims of their own greed and incompetence? What would our markets and industries look like without antitrust legislation? Would we want all the "jobs" free enterprise could produce if we eliminated the minimum wage?

Do we believe in the thousand points of light? Of course! How could we not, when their sparkle is all around us, the glittering panoply of generosity and voluntarism that lights up so many of our communities? The Red Cross, charities of every faith, volunteer firefighters, great philanthropists. All the people who reach out to help their fellow Americans recover from floods and earthquakes, and even from terrorism. Directly or indirectly, their light is reflected in each of our lives.

But we all know the truth: we will not come close to solving our huge national problems through the uncoordinated personal initiative of 250 million Americans. Private business can't afford to educate all the uneducated, or even all the people they need to hire! And education shouldn't be left in the hands of business anyway. No amount of private generosity could preserve the magnificence of our national parks or take sole responsibility for expanding the limits of our scientific knowledge. There is not enough heat in the thousand points of light to comfort all the shivering children. Not enough light to show the way home for all the people who have lost their way.

We need more than what each of us can do alone—and the Republicans have very little more to offer.

That's not to say the Republican agenda is devoid of merit. Some of their procedural reforms were long overdue. Requiring Congress to think more carefully about the impact of unfunded mandates on state and local government is good discipline and respectful of the federal-state partnership. Subjecting Congress to the same laws that everyone else must follow (such as those designed to protect workers from discrimination and other abuses) was only fair. Giving the President a line-item veto may help to curb pork barrel spending.

On the larger questions, however, like how to find employment for all our people and how to cure our social pathologies, their program is at best inadequate and in many respects actually harmful.

The Contract deals unsubstantially with our economic challenges. It tempts voters with tax cuts that appeal to our sweet tooth but won't build bone or muscle for the country. It's bursting with ideas to shrink the public sector but lacking in investments to grow the private sector. It appeals to the fears of people who feel wobbly about their economic future but offers no ideas for building a new American future on firmer economic ground.

With respect to our cultural problems, the Contract offers little more than castigation and negativism. It's all stick and no carrot, preaching without teaching. It encourages us to curse the darkness but doesn't inspire us to light candles. In the face of the profound negative forces that are burning away the country's soul, the Contract adds a negative jolt of its own. The result may be highly charged, but it will not be positive.

Moreover, the Contract would weaken us as a nation, ripping apart the ties that bind the citizens of each state to those of every other and insisting, as we yank open the plane door and leap into the twenty-first century, that this is the moment to trade our resilient federal parachute for fifty separate silk handkerchiefs. It's as if the Contractors think the Articles of Confederation would work better now than when we threw them out the first time back in 1789, having learned that thirteen states, operating largely independently with only the most tenuous connections, were not as good for our people as the closer knit union designed by the Constitution.

The Republican Economic Agenda

The Republican plan says tax cuts will do the stimulating we need to lift the economic tide and all our boats with it. In the 1980 campaign, candidate Ronald Reagan promised to cut taxes, increase defense spending, and balance the budget. And all of this on the theory, then unproven and now recently disproven, that cutting taxes was the route to national prosperity. Reagan's opponent in the primaries, George Bush, labeled this wishful thinking "voodoo economics." Predictably, the Reagan voodoo worked best for the rich, who gained most from the huge tax cuts. But it led to record deficits and to a widening gap between the rich and the rest of us. And its legacy of unprecedented peacetime deficits left the federal government without the money to make crucial public investments in people and infrastructure.

If we were surprised, we shouldn't have been; we had been

warned. Reagan's budget director, David Stockman, gloated that they had made unrealistic budget promises deliberately. He admitted that the Reagan plan was a Trojan horse designed to get people to accept massive tax cuts for upper-income Americans. The administration knew, and perhaps even hoped, that the flood of budgetary red ink would force cuts in the kind of social spending that conservatives saw as wrong.

The burden of debt bequeathed to us by the Reagan and Bush administrations makes it difficult for us to get a running start on the future by investing in the things we need. Through the first two centuries of the United States, encompassing thirty-nine Presidents and two world wars, we had accumulated less than $1 trillion in debt. It took voodoo economics only four years, the first Reagan term, to double that figure, and just twelve years to more than quadruple it. Now the annual interest on the debt drains money we need to invest in education, job training, and infrastructure, and to help our cities and states. It is a huge IOU that we are assigning to our children, who will have to repay it at great cost to their standard of living.

The new Republican Contract offers a virtually identical deception, featuring all the Reagan-era promises: cutting taxes, raising defense spending, and balancing the budget. It's nothing more than "déjà voodoo," only this time with a Gingrich scowl instead of the wonderful, reassuring Reagan smile. Democrats aren't the only ones who have noted the essential similarity. Jack Kemp actually called it *"Hoover* redux."

In the Reagan era, Republicans described their dance as "supply-side" or "trickle-down" economics, the theory being that if you gave tax breaks and other incentives to business and wealthy investors, business would prosper and investors would invest more, and the benefits would trickle down to the assembly-line workers and the rest of the middle class. The wealthy would keep most of the manna for themselves, but that would be okay, because they would scatter a little bit of it from their penthouses to the masses below. But the average American didn't experience any "trickle-down" benefits; many, in fact, got trickled upon. The new generation of Republicans are offering more of the same. I know what they would have said in my old neighborhood: "Fool me once, shame on you; fool me twice, shame on me."

What do we need to understand about the current Republican economic package? That however popular it may be, it won't deliver the short-term economic bonanza that is advertised and we will be paying a crippling bill for it for the rest of our lives, and the lives of our children. For the people who could really use some help, the Republican plan offers a sympathetic gesture but nothing significant, like throwing a cheery rubber duck to someone struggling to stay afloat. By contrast, for the strongest swimmers, our wealthiest individuals and corporations, the Republicans arrange a coast guard escort. And to the children of America trying to pull themselves through the rough waters of the coming century, the Contract comments coolly from the beach, "What a shame we can't afford to get you swimming lessons."

First, the rubber duck.

Promoters of the Contract are hoping that workers worried about an eroding standard of living and job insecurity can be mollified with tax cuts of varying size. They would create a $500-per-child tax credit and a complicated, gimmicky expansion of tax-sheltered Individual Retirement Accounts. The Republicans call it the "American Dream Restoration Act." Are our dreams that cheap—a tax break of $1.37 a day? Or is it just that Republicans, obsessed with the notion that they can attract voters by promising tax cuts no matter how imprudent, even dream of tax cuts in their sleep?

In the heyday of the urban political machines, precinct captains would deliver fresh turkeys to loyal voters in the old neighborhood, expecting gratitude for the gift to translate into votes for the party ticket. Today's Republicans use tax credits instead of turkeys. Newt Gingrich promises to deliver $500 or more to the doorstep of every family with children, in hopes they'll pull the Republican lever. The underlying strategy is identical to Reagan's 1981 tax cuts, and never was a larger turkey delivered to the American people!

Why? Because if you promise to cut taxes *and* balance the budget, the money has to come from somewhere. And if simulta-

neously you promise to keep your hands off the two biggest
government programs—Social Security and the Pentagon—the
money has to come from somewhere very painful indeed. In
effect, the Republicans leave themselves this choice: either they
pay for the tax cuts by cutting programs like Medicare far too
deeply—or they don't, and you do . . . but without really knowing what hit you.

Here's how it works: if they actually implement all the spending cuts that would be needed to pay for the tax cuts they propose, they will have to cut savagely into or forgo altogether
many of the investments that are the foundations for our future
—investments that would otherwise yield things like children
who can read, bridges that stand up, and new breakthroughs in
energy efficiency and environmentally sound technology. They
will also have to rip gaping holes in our social safety net, leaving
it in tatters, and leaving the most vulnerable among us out in the
cold. The cuts in Medicare and health care generally will leave
us unable to care for our sick and our elderly. In short, we would
enjoy a modest tax cut, but our children would be consigned
to underfunded, overcrowded schools and our aging parents
wouldn't have the nursing home bed or home health care they
need.

At the same time, we should brace ourselves for another inevitable Republican strategy, still bitterly familiar to anyone who
tried to balance a state or local budget during or after the Reagan
years: the Republican leadership will simply abdicate federal
responsibility for a host of problems, and casually shift the ever-
growing burden to the states.

The result? As state and local governments scramble desper-
ately to compensate for reduced federal assistance, they'll be
forced to hike their own taxes, replacing revenues collected
through the fairest and most progressive levy in the country, the
federal income tax, with revenues from sales and real property
taxes, which hit hardest at those least able to pay, particularly
those on fixed incomes. That's exactly what happened under
Ronald Reagan and George Bush, from coast to coast and at
every level of government. State and local sales taxes more than
doubled nationwide; property taxes nearly tripled.

On the other hand, if the tax cuts aren't fully paid for by cutting spending or saddling the states with new burdens, then the deficit will skyrocket. That will increase the debt burden on future generations. In effect, they're borrowing $500 from your children in order to give you a $500 tax cut! And a ballooning deficit tends to produce higher interest rates—which in turn slows down the economy, which in turn puts people out of work.

That won't happen, you say: "Haven't the Republicans already passed a plan to balance the budget, even with all the tax cuts?" Not really. All they have passed is a piece of paper that outlines the parameters of revenues and spending in years to come. Each year, the laws that impose the taxes, authorize the programs, and appropriate the actual funds will have to be passed by Congress and signed by the President. If recent history is any guide, the tax cuts will pass in a jiffy: tax cuts for individuals are a surefire way to win votes. But after an initial round of enthusiasm for spending cuts, paring down the budget will become more and more difficult, like trudging up a mountain path that grows increasingly steep and rocky. Constituents will applaud cuts they think will not affect them: everyone's for cutting the "fat." But when they're faced with the consequences of deeper and deeper cuts—cutting into the tissue and the muscle—they'll howl, as well they should, and they will demand an end to the mutilation and crippling of public services and programs. That's what happened after the initial burst of dramatic cuts during the first Reagan term. And that's what's already happening with the latest Republican plan. On paper, the deficits will come down, but they've set it up so that the dessert comes before the vegetables. Over the objections of more fiscally responsible members of their own party, the Contractors have insisted on initiating the tax cuts immediately, while deferring some of the harshest cuts in services to the later years of their seven-year syllabus.

Bad as Reaganomics was the first time, the consequences of this attempt to revive it will be a whole lot worse today. Since 1980, the national debt has more than quadrupled, we're more dependent on foreign capital, and the dollar is weaker. In that context, a soaring deficit now runs a high risk of driving us into what the noted economist and investment banker Felix Rohatyn has called "a brick wall of higher interest rates and a collapsing dollar."

All of that means we need to be very careful when the Republicans tell us about what's inside that beautiful heart-shaped box of tax breaks with our name on it, because now or later, one way or another, we foot the bill. That luscious federal tax break may be hard to remember after a couple of hideous new property tax bills, and it would be worth asking local governments if they think their constituents are in a mood to choose between higher taxes and giving up more than they already have in terms of education, local police, hospitals, and parks.

So much for the rubber duck.

Now for the coast guard escort: based on the Republican plans, households with yearly earnings above $200,000— roughly the top one percent of American earners—can expect an average tax cut of $16,500. Let's look at the centerpiece of the plan: the cut in capital gains taxes. That's the proposal to impose a lower tax rate on profits from the sale of assets like stock than we do on income like wages and salaries.

Is a capital gains cut effective in promoting economic growth? Maybe theoretically under exactly the right circumstances. But the last major capital gains tax cut was in August 1981, the first year of the Reagan supply-side experiment. Over the next two years, the economy grew by only one percent—a big drop from the 3.5 percent growth of the twelve months before the tax cut —and unemployment jumped from 7.3 percent to 9.3 percent! Conversely, the last major increase in capital gains taxes was 1986, as part of the Tax Reform Act. Over the next two years, the economy grew by 3.8 percent, much faster than the 2.2 percent growth of the twelve months before the tax hike, and unemployment dropped from 6.8 percent to 5.2 percent!

These facts don't prove that capital gains cuts hurt the economy: there were other factors at play. But it's important to understand that changing the tax rates on one type of income is like tossing a stone into the ocean of our $7 trillion economy: even if it's a big stone, the ripples are easily overwhelmed by the tides and currents of other economic trends. Even if it's a boulder, the resulting splash may be only temporary.

By the same token, however, it should be no surprise that lowering the capital gains rate doesn't seem to do much to boost the economy. The special preferences for capital gains have always covered existing investments as well as new ones. It's like General Motors announcing a rebate on Chevrolets to stimulate sales and then extending a rebate to all the Chevrolets already bought over the last twenty years! That would be a nice bonus for Chevrolet owners, but it would hardly be a rational, cost-effective way of spurring new car sales.

Besides, if the current tax rate on capital gains is such a burden on investors, how can you explain the fact that the stock market has spent the last few years leaping from one record-breaking pinnacle to another? Prior to 1987, the Dow Jones Industrial Average had never closed above 2,000; it reached the 3,000 milestone in 1991; 4,000 early in 1995; and soared above 4,500 by mid-1995.

On the other hand, it does seem clear that there are some dangers in cutting taxes if it's done at the wrong time. Reckless cuts can blast gaps in the federal budget. The Congressional Joint Committee on Taxation estimated that a capital gains cut like that proposed in the Contract with America would deprive the Federal Treasury of $47 billion over the first five years, and $208 billion over ten years. That would have to be added to the other business tax breaks already proposed, like tax deductions for corporate purchases of equipment, machinery, and buildings, which would drain nearly $170 billion over ten years. The Republican response has been to insist that Congress change the way tax changes are scored, or measured, by revenue estimators. That's about as fair as declaring that henceforward when your team scores a basket, it will count for ten points instead of the usual two. Again, it's déjà voodoo—"Let's take a gamble based on forecasting that cutting taxes will stimulate growth. If the gamble doesn't pan out . . . well, you're only short $10 or $20 billion, and you can always cut some benefits to children or the elderly to make up the difference."

As former Bush aide James Pinkerton says, what the Contract

is pushing is "essentially a pro-business agenda," under which "the top half of the economy will be liberated from government control," while little or nothing is done to help those in the bottom half. The Republican cup runs over with ideas for helping investors and business owners—but their cup is empty for workers. They proffer capital gains tax cuts but no education or skills training. They want government off the back of business but they won't give you government on the side of the people.

In an important sense their plan makes things worse for people at the bottom now—and for all of us later. Here's why. Although conservatives charge Democrats with fomenting "class warfare" (anytime we challenge a tax cut, for example), they are relentless in promoting their own brand of war between the classes. While praising the enterprise and initiative of the most powerful and successful parts of our nation, they steer the middle class's anger downward, toward those at the bottom of the economic ladder, arguing that they are the cause of our problems. They tell the white middle class, in so many words, "Your standard of living is threatened and your economic future insecure because America has been too generous to the poor." In subtle and not so subtle ways, they perpetuate the misleading stereotype that equates "poor" with "black or Hispanic welfare recipient," and they can be stunningly explicit in painting the scapegoats in colors—as when a conservative New York Republican said that "It's the blacks, the Hispanics . . . they are the people that got their hands out. They are the ones fighting for welfare." The truth is that millions of white people receive welfare, and millions of working people of all races are mired in poverty. More important, if anyone is responsible for the fading prospects of the middle class, it is surely not those Americans with the least money and power. They did not close the factories; they did not make the cynical fiscal judgments that have created the greatest debt and deficit in our history.

Then, building on the resentment they helped create, the conservatives propose to hornswoggle the middle class by saying: "Don't worry about your precarious perch or about the widening gap between you and the fortunate few above you. We'll just keep widening the gap between you and the unfortunate many below you." Of course, this doesn't make the middle class's position any less precarious. In fact, when you remove the safety net that cushions economic hardship, the fall will be even harder and more punishing for any who do lose their middle-class footing and slip down. It's just that if you push the poor down far enough, out of sight and out of mind, maybe the middle class won't notice how uncertain their own position really is.

The welfare question has taken on immense importance as a symbol. It is an expression of the turbulence battering the psyches of many Americans. It is a metaphor we like to brood over when we want to believe "the country is going to hell." But as we struggle to dance the right steps on the issue symbolically, we need to be clear about where this political tango will take us.

The welfare system does need serious and even radical correction, but we have to approach the process understanding in advance that neither the harshest nor the most innovative systemic reform will do much to improve our overall economic prospects—and that getting the welfare question wrong could hurt the nation and do real agonizing, irreversible damage to the lives of millions of our brothers and sisters who are poor.

The Unbalanced Approach to a Balanced Budget

By contrast, another conservative mantra, if carried to its logical conclusion, would have enormous consequences for the whole country: the obsession with balancing the budget by some arbitrary date no more than seven years from now.

Facing the immensely complex issues of federal budgeting and finance, congressional Republicans have tried to pare it all down to one simple maxim even Tarzan could understand: "Debt bad. Balanced budget good." Unfortunately, in the process of whittling a streamlined political decoy, they have scraped away the essential ideas and information that actually define the question at hand.

They say the federal government should balance its budget

the way a family balances its checkbook. But families take out mortgages to buy their homes and borrow to pay college tuition. They say the federal budget should be more businesslike. But businesses borrow money to build new plants. They say the federal budget should be balanced like the states' budgets. But most states take on debt by issuing bonds to pay for things like roads and bridges.

What they fail to say is that the federal government can't act more like these noble American institutions until it is more like them: until we redesign the federal budget to include a distinction any family or business could understand: the difference between current expenses and long-term investments, between groceries and a college education, between making payroll and building a brand-new plant, between those things you should never borrow to pay for and those where taking on debt is clearly an intelligent risk.

Believe it or not, this simple distinction doesn't exist in the federal budget, which means that for the moment insisting on perfect budget balance is both silly and self-defeating—as if a family tried to move up in the world by buying one semester of medical school for their oldest child, because that's all the cash they had on hand.

Even if the federal government were allowed to keep its operating and capital budgets in separate books, it's the height of hubris to assume that our economic forecasters and government budgeteers can shoot an arrow that will sail straight through seven years and trillions of dollars in economic activity, adjusting for interest rates and inflation and the impact of taxes on behavior and a hundred other variables that affect its flight, to land precisely on the bull's-eye of a balanced budget on September 30, 2002. Over each of the last twelve years, the federal government's forecast of the following year's budget has been off by an average of $42 billion—more than 20 percent. And it's not just a failing of government bureaucrats. Year after year, the top consensus forecasts of private economists prove wrong on everything from interest rates to GDP growth. (Perhaps that's why some wag once said that an economist demonstrates his competence not by making correct predictions but by explaining elegantly and cleverly why his previous prediction was wrong.) So let's be realistic. Of course we have to plan ahead. But let's not be led blindly into radical policy changes solely because we are dazzled by ephemeral projections about federal outlays equaling federal revenues seven years or a decade from now.

And let's not make a fetish out of balancing the budget. This may seem like heresy, but that only shows how much the notion of absolute balance has become unquestioned dogma. A much more realistic and sensible goal is to reduce the deficit, in a steady and reasonable way, so that the national debt grows at a rate slower than the overall economy, at the same time that we reorient more of what government does spend into investments that help the economy grow. We need to strengthen ourselves with fiscal restraint, not throttle ourselves with fiscal strangulation.

Despite these objections, it's easy to see how the rage for budget balance got started. More and more Americans lost patience with politicians sprawling around on both sides of the political aisle, dizzy with the pleasure of spending other people's money. By now, many Americans are so fed up that the only answer they seem satisfied with is the absolute one—zero tolerance for deficits. And they've embraced the notion that the way to achieve this beguilingly simple goal is to impose the heavy shackles of a constitutional amendment on our government. On the whole, members of Congress seem only too eager for the discipline of an amendment mandating a balanced budget: "Won't somebody stop us before we spend again!"

There's a problem, however, with using the Constitution as a spending cap—a problem that goes beyond whether lawmakers ought to have the backbone to restrain federal spending without leaning on the Constitution as a crutch. What's the goal of a balanced budget amendment? Presumably, to make sure that lawmakers don't write irresponsible budgets . . . but what if they do anyway? What if they try to evade the rules through budgetary gimmickry and fiscal sleight-of-hand; who would discipline Congress? Quite possibly nobody would, in which case the amendment would be a paper tiger, allowing all the fiscal indulgence in the current system, and in the process eroding the sanctity of the Constitution as a whole. The other alternative? The courts do the disciplining, just as they would if Congress passed a law that infringed on the constitutional guarantees of free speech or equal protection, in which case we would find ourselves asking un-elected judges with little or no experience in composing federal budgets to second-guess and overrule the people we did elect, in all the ten thousand separate decisions about revenues and outlays hammered out in budget making each year. That not only sounds like a bad idea, it would trample all over yet another vital constitutional principle known as the separation of powers.

There are a lot of reasons to be skeptical about a balanced budget amendment—but they are apparently not as enticing as all the political reasons to support it; enthusiasm for the concept has become virtually the price of admission to Republican and conservative circles of power in Congress. To start with, the proposal appears fiscally prudent, and that's always a good idea. It's popular with voters—another plus. And the pull is even stronger for some lawmakers, those whose goal in life is to dismantle social programs they disapprove of. For them, a balanced budget amendment looks like a dis-creet but iron-fisted way to force the people into accepting draconian spending cuts they would otherwise reject out of hand.

Disinvesting, the Republican Approach to Growth

I don't like the tactic of imposing a strict balanced budget re-quirement, and I'm surprised that the Republicans even think they need help in withholding spending: one of the gravest weaknesses of the Contract is that it "just says no" to spending on almost everything—except defense—no matter how clear the case that in several key areas we need to focus more money, not less.

For example, perhaps the best thing we could do right now

to improve people's lives and strengthen our free enterprise system is to invest intensively in human resources—public education, apprenticeships, job training, and so on. But the Republican agenda has hardly a word to say on the subject.

This is particularly ironic since Republican leader Newt Gingrich has been so vocal about the need to adapt to the emerging Information Age, when high tech and high skills will be the linchpins of the economy. He prophesies the coming of the so-called Third Wave economy in which the creation, manipulation, and distribution of information will supersede the manufacturing of products as the engine that drives economic growth. But he and his followers evidently don't see the need to help people prepare for this new era. As Secretary of Labor Robert Reich pointed out early on, the Contract with America does almost nothing to promote workforce skills, even though Newt Gingrich's futurist gurus preach that diverse and continually evolving skills are the essential element of the new information-based economy. The Republican agenda would actually cut back on education and job-training programs Americans sorely need to gird themselves for the future, leaving the glorious fruits of the new age to those with the private resources to acquire the special skills required.

Similarly, the Republicans apparently took one look at the homely subject of investing in our infrastructure and decided that they would rather rhumba with an issue that had some sex appeal—"Welfare reform! Now there's a knockout!" As a former governor, I know they are correct in assessing what's hot politically and what's not. No one ever comes up to you starry-eyed and says, "Oh, Governor, you *really* know how to structure the infra!" That is not, however, an excuse for ignoring such a profoundly important subject. From France to China, our competitors are spending billions to expand and upgrade their infrastructure, and unless we do the same, our economy will move ahead about as fast as a train that has run out of track.

In all these ways the Republican economic strategy is palpably inadequate and damaging, and in at least one other way it would actually do dramatic, and dramatically personal, harm. It all starts from the premise that American business is pinned to the ground by the combined weight of government regulation and private lawsuits.

Laws are what Congress passes; regulations are the practical rules government agencies create to translate the broad principles of law into the specific, enforceable details of day-to-day practice. Through a combination of bureaucratic rigidity, excessive moral zeal, and the accumulation of decades of piecemeal legislative and regulatory actions, a number of federal agencies have sprouted a tangled patch of these regulations. Increasingly, businesses snagged in the thorns have been complaining that much of it is confusing, expensive, burdensome, unnecessary, unproductive—even counterproductive.

Reaching once again for the Tarzan vote, Republicans growl, "Regulation bad!"—but instead of pushing for a top-to-bottom cleanup of a system that has gone a bit awry, they come as close as they dare to suggesting, "No more regulation ever." It's as if your house had become a little cluttered and sloppy, but instead of cleaning up the mess and throwing out the garbage, you simply declared that henceforth no one in the family would be allowed to put anything down on any horizontal surface without your written permission.

There's actually some poetic justice to the Republican strategy for stopping the flow of red tape: they propose to give regulators a taste of their own medicine by making it as arduous to impose regulations as it is to comply with them. In this case, however, poetic justice and real justice are not the same. The devil may dwell in the details of federal regulation, but the angels live there, too: the angels that swooped down in the twentieth century and for the first time offered us shelter from adulterated foods, shoddy building practices, dangerous toys, lethal working conditions, and unscrupulous employers. Yet the Republicans propose to subject environmental and health regulations to so-called cost-benefit and risk-assessment analysis that would deliberately bury federal agencies in so many new layers of red tape that virtually all new regulations would die before they were ever born. One version of the Republican assault on the ability of your government to protect health, safety, and the environment would build in more than sixty steps regulators would have to surmount to create any new rule.

If the Republican Contractors get their way, life will certainly be more irritating for regulators, but what about the rest of us? What are the likely consequences?

Here's one example: every year, five million Americans get violently ill because they unwittingly consume contaminated meat or poultry; four thousand of them die from it. Under Republican-backed measures, the Agriculture Department's efforts to modernize meat and poultry inspection procedures would be blocked, and restrictions on potentially dangerous pesticides and food additives would be eased. The result: more hamburgers will be contaminated, more lettuce will have pesticide residues, ketchup will contain additives that are now banned, and more Americans will be at serious risk. The Contract with America should carry a label: "Warning: Hazardous to Your Health. "

Through this and other measures, the Republicans in effect have offered business interests an all-you-can-eat buffet of bills that dismantle or weaken laws that protect the public interest. The current Congress has already made it much harder for an individual to sue a company, and their so-called takings bill, which would require taxpayers to pay businesses for the right to regulate them in the public interest, would create what the *New York Times* aptly called a "multi-billion-dollar welfare plan for corporations." Reporting on the first hundred days of the Gingrich-led House of Representatives, the *Wall Street Journal*'s headline read: "Business Is Big Beneficiary as 'Contract' Is Completed." The story begins: "Businesses struck it rich during the 100 Days; they're just not sure how rich."

Sidestepping Our Cultural Corrosion

The story is different for most Americans, of course. To the rest of us, including those whose daily lives are shaped by America's devastating social calamities, the Contract says, in effect, "Look, we can handle all our problems just by getting government out of the way and letting individuals fend for themselves." To the little boy let loose onto streets ruled by drug lords, to the pregnant sixteen-year-old, to the young man who knows his struggling school will never give him the skills to hold a real job, to the grandmother raising the child of the daughter she lost to crack cocaine—to all these despairing Americans, the Contract delivers this crude new ethic: "God helps those whom God has helped, and if God left you out, who are we to argue?"

It's familiar conservative economic thinking translated into the human sphere, a special brand of laissez-faire that might be known as "live and let die." Philosophically, it has always been popular with the winners in life, but even a child could tell you that it doesn't look anything like a solution, or even a real response, to our catastrophic social corrosion.

How would the Contract end drug abuse, or at least slow it down? How would it stop children from having children? Or roll back the tide of violence and crime? Apparently by brandishing the death penalty, more prisons, and longer sentences, while putting assault weapons back on the street; by cutting back on virtually every government program that helps people and cutting off welfare almost entirely; and by generally castigating all those people struggling in poverty.

The Contract says, in effect, "Let's get tough—really tough. Let's send them a message! That'll do it!" Really? As governor, I built more prison cells than all of New York's previous governors put together and raised the largest police force in our history. We spent billions more on criminal justice than ever before. I'll tell you, it was a heck of a message! But still, prisoners went into prison addicted and came out addicted—and went back to doing what they did before.

Despite all the evidence, despite what any parent could tell you, the Contractors nevertheless continue to believe that you can cure an addict with the hard end of a broom, or shout down the feelings of a teenager who thinks she needs a baby. Tell me, would you try it on your son, if he were alcoholic? Would it work?

In the end, what the Contract offers is nothing more helpful than a bitter chorus of negativism and castigation. Look at the question of violent crime, so bad for so long that people now find it both intolerable and deeply frightening, even when they don't live or work in the neighborhoods where the violence and disorder have become routine. The Republican response: "Build more prison cells!" But aren't these the same people who are so fond of observing that since the welfare system has its share of failures and doesn't seem to be solving the poverty problem, we should scrap it altogether? Over the past decade, we've built prison cells all across this country at such a pace that the construction alone has helped lift the economy in many places. We have a higher percentage of our population behind bars than any country on earth besides Russia—and yet most of us would say it hasn't made a dramatic difference in the rate of violent crime. By their logic, then, it would appear to be time to scrap the prison system. Believe me, I'm not suggesting it as an alternative, but neither am I ready to accept the false logic that promises a better America if only we had cages enough. Punishment is part of the answer, but it provides an incomplete solution without the kind of preventive measures that alleviate what used to be called the root causes and what still are the fundamental problems.

Their next strategy: "Kill the killers!" But killing killers has never deterred killing. Study the statistics in Texas, with the highest rate of executions and among the highest murder rates in the country. Ironically, if the tough guys are really interested in restraining government spending, they contradict themselves by heralding the death penalty. According to the latest estimates, it costs as much as two million dollars to catch, prosecute, and execute a murderer—significantly more than locking the criminal up for life! That's a high price to pay for revenge.

If signers of the Contract really wanted to do something about crime, they'd do something about the drugs and guns that make it such a bloody business. Instead, they want to undo the only real progress made on these problems in years: "Oh, by all means let's reverse the trend toward drug treatment! Let's reverse

the ban on assault weapons! Let's reverse the intelligent moderation of the Brady handgun law!" And they would do all this, the
new populists, even though it runs directly against what most
Americans ask for in the polls.

Or take the social problem Republicans love to hate more
than any other: illegitimate births to women on welfare. They
insist that an unwed mother with a young child should be
pushed promptly into the workforce, and that we should cut her
benefits if she has a second child while receiving government
help. Almost everyone would prefer to have the mother working,
including most of the mothers themselves. But where is she
supposed to work, exactly? If there were jobs in her neighborhood for unskilled teenagers, we wouldn't have an unemployment rate for high school dropouts in some places as high as 44
percent!

For the sake of argument, let's suppose that she can find a
decent job. Does making her work address the problem of the
irresponsible absent father? Does cutting off her benefits bring
him into the workforce or get him to help raise his children? Do
any of these responses help rescue the girl who saw so little
hope in her surroundings that having a baby seemed the most
powerful and consoling thing she could do?

Underlying all these approaches is another galling contradiction from the Undersecretaries of Family Values. If you're poor,
pregnant, and under eighteen, the Republicans insist from the
floor of Congress that the best thing for you and your baby is to
be separated all day, while you take whatever job you can get
and park the baby in whatever kind of marginal day care you
can possibly afford on your minimum wage. If they wouldn't let
their own grandchildren go through the door of a publicly
funded day care program, what makes them think that poor
children will come out of these overcrowded programs better off
than if we allowed their mothers to look after them at home?

Any honest assessment of the welfare problem suggests that
if we are to break the cycle of dependency, we will have to
invest in education, child care, health insurance, drug treatment,
and other services that enable the downtrodden to walk on their

own two feet. But the Republicans seem less interested in solving the problem than in scoring political points at the expense of people too weak to object effectively.

If the Contract's supporters are so interested in "sending a message" to the most troubled people in our society, they should be a little more careful about the signal their rhetorical e-mail is really flashing on the nation's screen. What message does it send when Senator Dole condemns the products of Hollywood fantasy as too depraved and violent, and at the same time urges us in real life to support the death penalty and allow easy access to assault weapons? That those things are apparently just exactly depraved and violent enough for his taste? What message does it send when Republicans suggest that we should offer our children better, more positive expressions of our culture, but then recommend that we cut funding for the Public Broadcasting System, the best source of wholesome educational programming for poor children, who need it most?

What message does it send when the Republican political agenda serves up, for the rich, juicy carrots like tax cuts but batters the poor with half a dozen heavy, hard sticks?

And when you tell a young woman on welfare that if she gets pregnant again, you won't help her support the child . . . what message does that send? That you hope she has an abortion? That it doesn't bother you if she runs out of food for her children before the end of the month? Or that, despite recent evidence to the contrary from a Republican-led state like New Jersey, you still believe this kind of harshness will keep poor women from having babies they can't afford?

If our leaders can't figure out how to keep their messages straight, they shouldn't be surprised if they don't achieve the results they're looking for. Actually, in terms of our social deterioration, it's an open question whether they're serious about getting results at all.

The one message that comes through from the Republicans in crisp bold type is that our problems seem too hard to solve, so they would prefer just to give up and walk away, to ignore them altogether or at least make clear that they don't see these questions as their responsibility. It's human nature. We don't like to feel stumped. We'd rather not be asked directions to a location we don't know how to get to. Thus, where there's no easy answer, the Republicans simply avoid asking themselves the question. In effect, their agenda builds an arch only partway across the chasm. And like a bridge that doesn't reach the other side, it's not only inadequate, it's dangerous.

And there is another kind of evasion going on. The Republicans have jumped aboard the latest trend in federal-state relations: "devolution." This is a fancy word that means shifting programs to the states on the theory that the states can do many things better and cheaper than the federal government. If the states, being closer to the front lines and more in touch with local needs, can make such good decisions, why not give them more discretion? Hey, if they save money while meeting basic needs, then we can decide how to share the savings! Sounds sensible, almost lofty. But we should always be suspicious when politicians appear to be giving away power—because it invariably means they are relieving themselves of responsibility in the process.

The Republicans claim they want to devolve welfare to the states because they believe the states have superior wisdom. But they don't hesitate to preempt the states in product liability, denying citizens remedies against corporations in state courts. They are destroying the federal safety net for needy families under the noble rubric of states' rights, while at the same time erecting a new federal safety net for negligent corporations by blithely supplanting state law.

At the moment, the states get money from Washington for programs like Medicaid and Aid to Families with Dependent Children according to need: if more people are down on their luck where you live because of a regional recession, the federal government sends your state a bigger check. In exchange, every state agrees to follow certain rules—providing a certain range of benefits and services to set categories of people. In recent years, some states have started to complain that the federal guidelines are too rigid, or even irrelevant—that the needs of the single mother in East Los Angeles are so different from those of the elderly couple in rural Louisiana that the states should be given much more power to design the right answers for themselves. Not a bad premise, but what do the states have to accept in exchange for the freedom? A lot less money. Under devolution, federal aid would be doled out in block grants of a fixed amount that would stay the same in good times and bad, and regardless of whether a local plant laid off two hundred people or twenty thousand. Whatever happens, the state would have to make up the difference.

Devolution is one way to describe it: abdication of responsi- bility is another. Again, we see a repeat of the Reagan experi- ment, under which states and local governments were given a smaller share of the federal budget, and bore more of the burden of meeting domestic needs.

Moreover, if we saddle the states with responsibility for the social safety net, we run the risk that state budget making will degenerate into a welfare cutting contest, pitting each state against all the others, with the poor taking all the punishment. Left to their own devices, and with a responsibility to balance their own budgets, states have a strong incentive to discourage the have-nots and attract the haves. Haves are partial to tax cuts —so why not pay for a tax cut by slashing the size of your welfare checks? Who's going to notice if that leaves the poor even further behind? It's also a fact that the record of some states in protecting children is a sordid one. Thousands of children in state-run so-called child protective services have died of abuse and neglect. Nearly two dozen states are under court order to improve their protective obligations to children. In the end, as the federal government and then the states snip holes in their social safety nets, the problems fall squarely into the lap of the inner cities, which don't possess the resources to deal with them. This is a recipe for social disaster.

Perhaps the most troubling aspect of devolution is what it says about us as a nation. Are we to erode the notion of our rights and obligations as Americans, and think of ourselves primarily as residents of Kansas or New Jersey, no longer bound to one another as fellow citizens of the United States? When the Senate Finance Committee voted to turn welfare completely over to the states, with federal funding capped rather than guaranteed as an entitlement, and with no requirement for states to match the federal payments, Father Fred Kramer, president of Catholic Charities USA, described it as a disaster for children. Senator Carol Moseley-Braun cut to the heart of the matter: "We are deciding whether or not these United States are one country or a conglomeration of fifty separate entities. Under this bill, if children wind up sleeping in the streets in one state, there is nothing the rest of the country can do about that."

A Political Coup, a Practical Disaster

It's not surprising that the GOP plan comes up so short substantively. It's composed of simplistics, emotionalism, shibboleths, and empty slogans that appeal to the worst that is in us. It is a kind of plastic populism that will bend or break when tested with the full weight of our real problems. It doesn't hold up to logical analysis. In some places, it doesn't even *seem* to make good sense—except perhaps politically, where, in a cynical way, it suggests to hard-pressed middle-class Americans that their tax dollars are being wasted in futile "do good" programs. The constant drumbeat about the crisis of children living with only one parent is part of that pretense. Of course a child is better off with two loving, responsible parents, but studies show that many outcomes are related more to the presence or absence of poverty than to the presence or absence of both parents. For example, children living with only one parent are somewhat more liable to drop out of school than children from intact families, but children living in poverty are over three times more likely to drop out than the nonpoor.

The Republican agenda is also bursting with inconsistencies and outright hypocrisy. It commends churches and other nonprofit groups as the institutions best suited to help the needy, yet it proposes to slash the government funding they rely on. And despite their putative regard for religious institutions, the Contract's supporters turn a deaf ear to pleas by religious leaders like

Cardinal John O'Connor and the Catholic bishops not to dismantle social programs. They ignore the clear evidence from the
people who actually run the charities that even the very best
efforts of the most generous philanthropies are no substitute for
government in trying to meet the most basic needs of millions of
vulnerable Americans.

Government revenues account for 17 percent of the Salvation
Army's budget and two-thirds of the budget of Catholic Charities
USA, a network of about 1,400 social service agencies. On average, 40 cents out of every dollar budgeted by private nonprofit
organizations engaged in human services comes from the government. Less than one-fifth of wealthy Americans surveyed said
they would make larger charitable contributions if the government slashed social spending. Adjusted for inflation, charitable
contributions have risen only slightly over the last ten years. And
much philanthropic giving is to institutions patronized by the
wealthy themselves—museums, symphonies, their collegiate
alma maters, and the like—rather than to social services for
the poor. You'll find a lot more private college dormitories and
symphony halls than homeless shelters named after wealthy
philanthropists. Adding irony to injury, many of the loudest Republican voices in favor of relying on private charities also advocate drastic changes in the tax code, such as switching to a flat
rate tax or a consumption tax, that would remove or reduce the
income tax break that currently gives donors an extra incentive
to give.

The Republicans engage in government bashing and call
shrilly for smaller government. Yet they suggest government
should get into the child-rearing business through orphanages.
They rail against "big government," but they launched one of
the biggest bureaucracies in history, the Resolution Trust Corporation, to deal with the savings and loan mess. They support
government subsidies for water and wheat. They're willing to
have government intrude in the bedroom and in the relation
between a woman and her doctor. And they call for a larger
defense budget. It's only when the government serves other
people that it's too much and too big.

Then there's their hypocrisy on term limits. To ride public

anger into power, Republicans promised to make term limits a political commandment: "Thou shalt throw the bums out" every six years. Now that they're the "bums," they seem to have lost their religion on the subject, a syndrome that affects both parties when they are exposed to the temptations of power.

After campaigning as outsiders who would return control of the government to the people and away from the special interests, they've transformed themselves with lightning speed into the same kind of consummate Washington insiders the Democrats were for so long. Rather than implement lobbying and campaign reforms, they've used their new positions of power to solicit massive donations from Washington lobbyists. During the first two months of 1995, the Republican National Committee raised more money, primarily from corporate contributions, than it did during the entire previous nonelection year. As the *New York Times* reported, Republicans have not only been hitting up lobbyists for funds, they are actually punishing lobbying firms that hire people who fail their ideological litmus tests. Especially disturbing is the blatant way in which they have pandered to industry lobbyists. The Republican House leaders invited gaggles of corporate lobbyists into their congressional suites to collaborate, behind closed doors, in drafting federal legislation to gut safety and environmental regulations. These same Republicans, without a hint of shame, accuse advocates for things like child nutrition programs of representing "special interests."

In fact, one of the few times congressional conservatives buck the opinion polls is when the issues at stake are near and dear to their favorite special interests. "Courageously," they disregard public support for higher taxes on the rich, gun control, lobbying restrictions, women's right to choose, and lower defense spending.

Senator Phil Gramm recently complained that the problem today is a "government that rewards us when we fail and taxes us when we succeed." Doesn't that complaint sum up the Republican idea in a nutshell? Government, one must infer, ought to give to those who have already succeeded and take from those who fail! Presumably, government aid should go not to the destitute, the disabled, the disadvantaged, but to the fit and the fortunate, the oil tycoon, the stock investor, the already strong and mighty, on the dubious grounds that this will strengthen the society.

The Republicans' agenda is rooted in misconceptions and a willful refusal to face reality. They marched into office under the banner of a balanced budget and a new round of middle-class tax cuts. They trumpeted the spending cuts that hurt poor children, immigrants, and welfare mothers—people who generally can't or don't vote. None of their bright banners displayed the cuts they planned that would hurt the middle class. Not one of them campaigned on the platform, "Elect me and we'll slash $270 billion from Medicare! Vote for me, and I promise to shut down Amtrak and sell off national parks and curb financial aid to college students!" Now that they're in power, and the rest of us are starting to grasp the true magnitude of their budget-cutting proposals—the most draconian reductions in worthwhile services for Americans that the nation has ever seen—they deny that their middle-class constituents will feel the sting. "No, really, it's a great system," they contend. "We take away your cake, and you can still eat it, too." And they continue to try to mislead us about the biggest government program of all, Social Security, privately conceding the system is headed for crisis but unwilling to confront it publicly because it would be politically inconvenient to do so.

The Contract plays on popular fears and misconceptions, speaking indignantly about the cost of AFDC and foreign aid as if these programs were the primary cause of our fiscal distress, when each accounts for only about one percent of the federal budget. It also exploits the latest wave of anti-immigrant sentiment, born as always of economic uncertainty, but ignores data that show immigrants overwhelmingly contribute to, not drain, our economy.

Much of the Republican attack is aimed at a variety of New Deal and Great Society social programs that were designed to protect Americans from the kind of desperate poverty still prevalent in much of the rest of the world. The signers of the Contract make the fatuous argument that since we've had programs like

welfare for decades and we still have social problems, the programs not only didn't solve the problems but helped cause them,
and so we should throw them out. That's absurd. You can't
blame a problem on the attempt to solve it. That's like blaming
the Band-Aid for the wound. Their syllogism makes no more
sense than saying that we've tried capitalism for two hundred
years and we still have poverty, so we should scrap the free
enterprise system, or that we gave the Catholic Church two thousand years to wipe out sin and they haven't quite done it, so the
pope should just fold up his Basilica and go home.

Besides, the facts simply do not support the effort to link our
social problems with the rise of welfare programs. Out-of-
wedlock birth rates rose from the mid-1960s onward, after the
Great Society's expansion of social programs; but they were rising before that period as well. They continued to climb through
the 1980s, even as the real value of welfare benefits dropped.
Today, they are rising throughout the world, even in some of the
former communist nations that have begun the transition from
socialism to free market economies. Finally, if welfare benefits
spur out-of-wedlock births, you'd expect the states with the most
generous welfare benefits to have the highest illegitimacy rates.
In fact, the opposite is true, and illegitimacy rates are highest in
states like Mississippi and Texas, which pay among the lowest
benefits in the nation. If you need further proof, a nonpartisan
study recently concluded that, contrary to early claims, New
Jersey's highly touted policy of denying additional benefits to
mothers who have babies while on welfare has had no discern-
ible impact on their birth rates.

The Republicans are so determined to do things differently,
to shake things up, to grab attention, that they often wind up
suggesting things that are downright silly. Like House Speaker
Newt Gingrich proposing a tax credit for poor people to buy
laptop computers. Trying to spread computer literacy is a worthy
goal, in fact an essential one. But a tax credit means an amount
you can subtract directly from the taxes you would otherwise
owe. Since most of the working poor pay virtually no taxes
already because of the Earned Income Tax Credit, and since the
poorest of the poor, like those on welfare, don't earn enough

income to owe any taxes at all, how would a new tax credit help them?

The Gingrich idea, which he himself conceded was a bit "nutty," also highlights the Contractors' obsession with primitive individualism. He'd prefer to call for a government program that gives each individual his or her own computer than to support funding levels for public schools and libraries that would ensure these public facilities have adequate computers and the staff to teach the kids how to use them.

For all its shortcomings, however, the Republicans' stark agenda forces us to confront some fundamental questions about the role and scope of government in our third century of nationhood. The issues are on the table: Should our government maintain a social safety net that guarantees bare sustenance to all, or should we simply let the unfit fall to the hard ground below? Can government help the economy, or should it just get out of the way? Do the poor deserve our help or don't they? Should the edifice of our strong federal government be dismantled? What does it mean to be the *United* States, anyway? And perhaps most important, what are our obligations to one another? Is individualism the key that unchains our spirit or the knife that cuts out our heart?

These questions are profound, and worth addressing, but the answers surely do not lie in abdicating our responsibility for each other. President Kennedy told us: "Ask not what your country can do for you. Ask what you can do for your country." The Republican slogan seems to be "Ask only what you can do for yourself." That's not enough to ask of ourselves. The Republicans talk of the future, but would have us revert to the past, to a more primitive time when it was every man for himself and only the strong survived. They speak of the "opportunity society," but for millions of Americans they would slam the doors of opportunity shut. They mouth the language of hope, but they offer policies of despair. They boast of a strong America, but their agenda is premised on the defeatist attitude that America is not strong enough, wise enough, or great enough to help more people succeed than are currently succeeding. They act as though we have lost our ability to help one another grow to our full capacity. They claim that they are "revolutionaries" committed to "renewing America," but the harm caused by their spending cuts will be severe in many cases, meaning for some even the difference between life and death, and for the rest of us benefits that will at best be dissipated and marginal. They sing the hymns of family values, but their policies favor profits over people every time.

There is a better way.

4

Going Forward
Together

——

I have tried in the preceding chapters to describe where America seems to be, and seems to be heading—and the news is not all good. That's true not only for individual Americans and our common culture and economy, but also for our political system as a whole. With every new election, it seems, more of us than ever choose to bow out of our roles as citizen voters. Part of the reason is the nature of today's political debate, too often reduced to a relentless exchange of negativism, distortions, and slogans. The Republican favorite at the moment appears to be "Government is no good and it's certainly too big."

But this complaint is meaningless in the abstract. Too big for what? No good for what? And in order to answer these questions, we must first understand what it is we are trying to achieve through our government and what functions we believe our government ought to perform. This inquiry should start with one rock-hard, fundamental principle upon which all of our future will be built. It is an idea that transcends party labels and narrow ideologies. It is an idea different from the macho individualism advocated by the Republicans—a stronger, sounder, and sweeter one. It is the idea of community.

The Idea of Community

Contestants in the last few elections have tried to attract attention to themselves with some flashy positions on the subject of "family values." Although in the hot light of a press conference these gaudy arguments glitter like the real thing, I have always thought they were costume jewelry, standing in for the real fight we were too afraid to have, the fight over much larger questions: Who are we as a people? What ultimate values inform our individual souls? What values, if any, configure our soul as a nation?

This desire for definition is really the story of America—from the self-evident truths of the Declaration of Independence through Lincoln's words in the Civil War; from the poetry of Walt Whitman and the stories of Mark Twain to the paintings of Edward Hopper; from the fear of communism to the protests over Vietnam—the perennial quest for identity of a nation without a bloodline.

For our first century and a half, we could have defined ourselves as a nation of individuals driven by three principal ideas:

Opportunity. Each of us is entitled to the chance to work and to succeed on our own merits, regardless of birth or background —still a revolutionary idea in human history.

Liberty. Each of us has the right to choose our own path in the world, as long as we do no harm to our fellow citizens; the right to believe what we want to believe, and say so; the right to worship any god, or no god; the right to feel safe in our own neighborhood or any other.

Responsibility. Each of us has the obligation to work if we can; to care for our children, and for our parents when the time comes; the obligation to obey the law, pay our bills, pay our taxes, pull our own weight.

These ideas have united Americans since before we were a

country, but at one point in our changing history, while clinging
to them as fundamental propositions, we began to see that although individualism might be all-American, it was not all
America needed. As we grew and industrialized, we continued
to cherish the strength of our democracy, our spirit of initiative
and personal drive, our sense of daring and capacity for innovation, but we recognized that if we limited ourselves to old-
fashioned individualism, we would be limiting our nation's
strength and our chances for progress. Seeing all this, we added
one more powerful principle that subsumed all the others and
that helped us create the most successful nation in world history:
the idea of community, as encouraged and promoted through
our participation in government.

Community, added to individualism, brought us unprecedented strength, the strength of a diverse group of people setting
aside their lack of shared blood, faith, traditions, and hierarchies
to work together for the common good. This commitment may
appear a bit tenuous from time to time in today's America, but it
is the spirit that energizes us instantly in crises: Midwest floods,
West Coast earthquakes, and East Coast hurricanes; disorienting
acts of terrorism, whether aimed against the bustle of New York
or the calm of Oklahoma City. It's the spirit that pulled us out of
the Great Depression and lifted us to victory in World War II.
And it is also the intelligence that has helped distinguish the last
sixty years of American history from those that came before, as
we have tried, in fits and starts, to look out for one another more
dependably, through our government, from Social Security to
civil rights.

When the danger is clear and present, we pull together su-
perbly. But in the intervals between crises, our strong streak of
individualism often overpowers us and encourages us to behave
as though we were capable of surviving and thriving as 250
million disassociated entities.

You cannot have been in politics as long as I have and be
blind to the fact that for most of us, most of the time, self-interest
is a powerful motivator—perhaps the most powerful one. If we
hope to reestablish our strength, confidence, and balance as a
nation, we need to help one another see that our self-interest is

not identical with our selfish interests, that self-interest is inextricably linked to the common good. We need to understand that apart from the morality of recognizing an obligation to our brothers and sisters, common sense by itself should teach us that we are all in this thing together, interconnected and interdependent. Even if your two-parent family is safely ensconced in the suburbs, happily employed, financially comfortable, well educated, well insured, young, healthy, able, and free of drugs, it's in your self-interest for government to help those people who are not as successful as you. In part of course that's because someday you may, one way or another, be among the vulnerable ones. Who among us is insulated perfectly against losing a job or being crippled in a highway crash? Against catastrophic disease, addiction, divorce—or growing old?

But beyond this calculation of our own potential vulnerabilities, there are other reasons to think that working to strengthen all parts of our society serves our own individual interest. Perhaps you think government shouldn't have to pay for welfare, Medicaid, drug abuse treatment, job training, public schools, or assistance to the homeless. Maybe you think we should cut back on all these expenditures, because you'd appreciate paying less. Think about it a little longer, though, and you'll see that things don't work that way. The truth is, where these programs don't already exist or are inadequate or underfunded, what we "save" in government outlays we simply pay for in another way—in part by exacting the cost in a thousand regrettable adjustments in our daily lives.

You pay for it every second of the sixty-minute commute you're stuck with because there's no place safe to live in the city anymore. You pay for it when your company can't find workers literate enough to do the job, when you feel forced to send your child to private school, when the premium on your health insurance keeps shooting upward to pay for all the people with no coverage at all. You pay for it when you choose to take a taxi instead of the subway to avoid explaining to your little daughter why, if that man lying on the platform is so cold, he can't just come home with you.

And in the hidden ways we pay the price together, the costs

are just as painful. It would be nice if we really loved one another. But even if we cannot bring ourselves to love the strangers who are failing, we have to understand that as a matter of self-interest, we can no longer afford the terrible cost of our social failures. We cannot afford the cost of more and more police and prisons, of welfare and AIDS babies, of gun violence and overflowing emergency rooms. The country cannot afford, in this ever more competitive world, the price of opportunity lost —the opportunity for stronger workers, expanding markets, growing productivity. Our future will not bring us a rising standard of living unless we raise the living standards of all Americans.

Would you like more evidence? Consider a few facts.

- Childhood poverty is rising steadily in the United States, but every single year that it simply continues at current levels, the educational and social failure results in an estimated future loss to our nation of $177 billion in economic output.
- When people with no health insurance turn to hospital emergency rooms for their primary medical care, it typically costs more than twice as much to treat them than if they had their own doctor and proper insurance.
- Crime costs our society $165 billion a year. That's the sum of all the police, the prisons, the court costs, private security, injuries to victims, and the value of stolen property.
- A number of economists have concluded that quite apart from any moral considerations, too large a gap between the rich and the poor, as we have in America today, actually hurts the overall economy. Over the last two decades, for example, metropolitan areas with the largest gaps between central city and suburban incomes lagged far behind those with less inequality. It's like a car whose tires are of such wildly different sizes that the vehicle can't drive straight.

Or translate that impact into individual terms. Let's say you're a busy owner of a small hardware store. Knowing that you can't offer the rock-bottom prices of the huge discount houses, you emphasize service to the customer. You want to hire some entry-level employees. You're willing to train them, but they need to be able to read instruction manuals, take measurements, and handle inventory. You find that recent graduates from your local high school lack basic math and reading skills. So whom are you going to hire?

You want to provide health insurance to your employees, not only because you think it's fair but because you have to offer competitive benefits to hold on to your best workers. But you find that you can't afford it; insurance premiums are too high because hospitals and doctors have had to raise the fees they charge their insured patients in order to offset the losses they suffer from caring for the 40 million uninsured Americans.

Your store stays open most evenings, and you're particularly concerned about crime after dark. A young man addicted to crack mugs a customer leaving the store one evening. The bad publicity drives other customers away. A few months later, some other criminals break into your storage area, stealing thousands of dollars of inventory. Finally, you yourself are held up at gunpoint while working the cash register—and you decide to close the store.

If we want to keep America open for business, we need not a return to the primitive individualism of our frontier days but a new sense of national community.

Where will we find it? Not in the Constitution, not even in the Bill of Rights; we have no federal constitutional right to, say, food stamps or unemployment insurance. The closest we come is in the Preamble, with this triumph of hopeful vagueness: to "promote the general welfare." Our Constitution is designed to protect individual liberty better than any other document ever dared to—but it does not ask us to join together, to share intelligently, to love.

In fact, for the first two-thirds of our history, that was true of our laws in general—they contained little to suggest how much we really need one another. There were exceptions, like the homesteads and land-grant colleges created by Congress in the mid-nineteenth century. But on the whole, the proposition that government should help people help themselves, and should take care of those who couldn't, was not a matter of broad agreement.

Especially after the Civil War, what we now call social Darwinism reigned as the dominant social philosophy, its doctrines squaring solidly with the business interests of the day. But then the abuses began to surface—the ruthless predatory Mr. Hyde heart inside the magnanimous, moralizing Dr. Jekyll that was the Industrial Revolution. With immigrants streaming in from everywhere, there were hundreds of thousands more Americans than ever, and more of us were working than ever—but in circumstances of unprecedented, almost medieval misery. Child labor. Twelve- and fifteen-hour days. Working conditions so wretched—from the sweatshops and steel mills to the tobacco fields, railways, and mines—that just by going to work you might risk blindness, deafness, mutilation, disease—and even death, like the dozens of young seamstresses who died in the appalling Triangle Shirtwaist Factory fire in lower Manhattan in 1911, before there were building codes to save them. Wages were so pitiful that thousands of families were pushed into desperate debt to their own employers, who sold them the necessities of life on credit but at inflated prices. A protest song of a slightly later era explained it this way: "St. Peter, don't you call me, 'cause I can't go; I owe my soul to the company store." And at the end of their shifts, what awaited the workers at home? The overwhelming squalor of the terrifying new slums. Although America had no shortage of moral authorities, from powerful churches to horrified philanthropists, none of them, it appeared, had the power to stop the brutality and aggressiveness of a system driven purely for profit.

By the late nineteenth century, the populist movement reared up as an inevitable response, followed, in the early morning of the new century, by progressivism. As historian Richard Hofstadter has written, populism was the first political movement to "insist that the federal government has some responsibility for the commonweal . . . the first such movement to attack seriously the problems of industrialism." As populist enthusiasm grew, America's faith in laissez-faire shrank in proportion, clearing the way for the new view that the central government could and should play a definite role in the nation's economy.

Throughout the period, the populists were vehement on one point: that their purposes chimed in perfect harmony with those laid out in the Constitution: "to form a more perfect union," to "promote the general welfare," and so on. Declaring in their first party platform that "this Republic can only endure . . . while built upon the love of the people for each other and for the nation," they allowed themselves to aspire boldly for America:

> We believe that the power of government—in other words, of the people—should be expanded . . . as rapidly and as far as the good sense of an intelligent people and the teachings of experience shall justify, to the end that oppression, injustice, and poverty shall eventually cease in the land.

Suddenly, all kinds of change was thinkable. Progressives like Louis Brandeis, the influential legal scholar and "People's Attorney" who later served on the Supreme Court, could advocate the use of federal power to support the interests of the disadvantaged. The federal government began taking steps to break up or at least regulate the monopolies and trusts whose economic tyranny was deemed damaging to democratic capitalism. As the century progressed, so did the thinking, and other leaders—Al Smith from the rough streets of New York City, Franklin Roosevelt from the serene reaches of the Hudson—began to imagine a recipe for a sweeter America than we had ever tasted before. By 1938, New York State would actually have a new constitution that explicitly stipulated a state responsibility for the poor.

They were good ideas from the start—and the Depression made them indispensable in all their manifestations, from Social Security and unemployment insurance to Aid to Families with Dependent Children. In important ways, the rest of this century has been a chronicle of how America has used her government to build on this robust and largehearted spirit of national community, from World War II, to the War on Poverty, to the civil rights revolution.

What we need now is not to kill that spirit, as the conservative

Republicans propose, but to revive it—and make it an active clause in what the late Gunnar Myrdal once called "The American Creed."

Myrdal observed that, historically, America has always been more than an assortment of individuals because of this extraordinary fact: regardless of our race, religion, or class, we are held together by a bond of powerful ideas, an amalgam of the "ideals of the essential dignity of the individual human being, of the fundamental equality of all men, and of certain inalienable rights to freedom, justice, and a fair opportunity." This creed, said Myrdal, is the "cement in the structure of this great and disparate nation." Without that cement—the shared commitment to these ideals—much of what we think of as "America" dissipates. The United States of America stops being a daring experiment in democratic rule and starts being just another spot on the map.

So—how can we transform this noble philosophical bond into a practical change in attitudes and actions, particularly in an age when even the simple habits that connect us to our neighborhoods and hometowns are fading? As Robert Putnam of Harvard has pointed out, factors like the recent retreat to the cocoon of nuclear family and infinite options for electronic home entertainment have created a self-reinforcing pattern of autonomy bordering on isolation. More Americans bowl than ever— but fewer and fewer bowl in leagues. More of us listen to classical music but very few of us do it together in concert halls. Sadly, as we cease to be in contact with one another, we actually cease to want the contact, with all the compromise and conflict it entails. I believe a crucial part of changing that pattern and creating national community will be putting an intense national focus on rebuilding the habits of a healthy democracy.

Although a willingness to offer the helping hand of government to those in need is part of what I mean by a sense of national community, it's not the only thing. I also mean what we called civics when I was in high school. All too often these days, we either make demands upon government as though we were irate customers jostling for service in a crowded restaurant, or we hurl abuse upon government as though we were rowdy spectators at a hockey game. Civics implies a recognition that we are more than customers or spectators of our government; that we—the citizens—have responsibilities to one another in the public sphere; and that democratic self-government presupposes the people meet their civic duties.

Civic duties? What the heck are those? Most Americans used to know, but today, few of us feel that "citizenship" is our personal obligation. Unfortunately, that alienation from government is another self-reinforcing tendency toward self-defeating isolation—and worse. Consider this: we are witnessing in this country two simultaneous trends that should be contradictory but apparently are not. Many Americans are howling that their lawmakers should be limited to shorter terms—too short to make much trouble, they say, and who cares if they're also too short for anyone to gain any real expertise? At the same time, faced with the disconcerting complexity of so many policy issues—health care reform comes to mind—more and more people have given up pretending to follow it all and have just stopped voting. But if our elected representatives become as transient as college students and we the people can't be bothered anymore, who are we leaving in charge of our national community—career bureaucrats, veteran congressional staff, and well-connected special interest lobbyists, none of whose "terms" is limited? We have to find a better answer than that.

With their drumbeats of criticism against virtually everything government has done or attempted with the exception of military exploits, the apostles of the New Harshness have certainly not contributed to a revival of the civic duty to participate in our own governance, despite their generalized flagwaving. But they are not the only element of our society that pays insufficient heed to the importance of community. The freewheeling, if-it-feels-good-do-it, self-actualizing, personal-liberation ethos that captured the imagination of so many young people starting in the 1960s also fuels a narcissistic individualism that pulls us apart rather than together. "I do my thing and you do yours; and if by chance we meet, it's beautiful," went a popular saying of the time, as though each of us dances through life free-form by ourselves, and only by happenstance crosses the other dancers'

paths—rather than learning to coordinate our steps with a part-
ner, as in old-fashioned ballroom dancing, or with a group of
friends and neighbors, as in traditional folk dancing.

This same self-indulgent individualism is manifest every day
in our commercialized, consumerist world: "Get the newest, fastest car!" "Pamper yourself with lotions and perfumes!" "Thirsty?
Don't be satisfied with a simple glass of water—indulge your
sweet tooth and gulp some soda—and not just any soda, but
'gourmet' soda!" "Solve your problems by ordering this gadget
or that gizmo—operators are standing by!"

We need to do all the time what we do so well when catastrophes loom—we need to look outside ourselves and to reestablish a sense of community, both in our daily lives and in the way
we view our government. We need to understand and fulfill our
civic responsibilities at the same time that we seek to gratify our
personal needs and desires. We need to appreciate and respect
the rights of others at the same time that we insist on exercising
our own rights and freedoms.

Reestablishing this vision must be a major focus for America
for the next decade or more. A new sense of national community
will help us advance our nation economically, help alleviate our
social ills, and reinvigorate our cherished political system.

Without that sense of community, we will be defenseless
against politicians who offer wedges instead of solutions. We
will move deeper into the dark woods of either/or, in which
every debate is painted as a contest between good and evil,
in which compromise and rational discussion become impos-
sibilities.

Without community, without a sense of our common interest,
we will cede to those infinitely organized and articulate voices
called the special interests the strength and wealth of this nation.

Without a sense of community—without a restoration of those
powerful unwritten codes of conduct that prevent more law-
lessness than the law ever could alone—we will begin the steady
march toward a society in which we are forced, bit by bit, to give
up our freedoms so that "someone from the government" will
take care of those scary kids on the corner.

Without community, we can bid good-bye to the "tradition"

of American prosperity. Because we cannot make it as a nation if we lose a generation of our children to drugs, or AIDS, or inadequate education—even if they're not your children, or mine. We cannot survive without their talent and intelligence and energy. We cannot afford to jam our prisons and leave our laboratories half-empty. We cannot make it if we fail to rescue those who've been left behind.

Those of us who are comfortable may run away from the consequences for a while. We can move to pretty, impenetrable suburbs, or marble fortresses with doormen who look like Swiss Guards, or even into planned communities that in their quest for perfect isolation indulge in every strategy short of a drawbridge and a moat. But eventually, we will run out of places to hide, and then we will understand what we might have understood before: that no man is an island. No woman. No race. No region, state, or neighborhood. For all our macho individualism, we cannot make it as individuals alone. In this complex and inter-connected democracy, we will each find our individual good in the good of the whole community. I must think of the jobless father in Brooklyn as my father—the struggling young mother in rural Georgia as my own. Not my blood, not my neighborhood, not my color, perhaps—but my child. It is still the biggest and most useful truth—for us to succeed as a society, we must come together, recognizing that we must be the family of America; that in the end, we are bound to one another—because it is right and because it is necessary.

It is also the ancient wisdom. The Hebrew sages told the Jews that their role in life is to repair the entire universe . . . *tikkun olam*. Christians are taught that their task is to complete God's work in the world, that we are all, no matter how small, "collabo-rators in creation."

Applying these truths to our private lives and our public poli-cies will give America the heart to aspire more boldly and the strength to achieve those aspirations. Equally important, the gen-tle idea of community can help us fill the aching void in our national soul, a void we are struggling now to hide under a fierce mask of harshness and outrage. A commitment to the whole community of people around us can dissolve the walls of isola-

tion and separateness that hold us back. Because ultimately it
is self-defeating to try to achieve happiness through personal
gratification alone: Which cake is more delicious? The one you
bake and eat all by yourself, or the one you prepare for a party
of friends and loved ones?

Most of us eventually conclude that lasting happiness requires
a belief in something larger than ourselves. Listen to the senti-
ments of a Virginia man who explained why he dove into a river
to rescue a stranger in a sinking car: "I just couldn't watch the
guy drown. I think I jumped into the water out of self-defense. I
wouldn't have been able to live with myself if he had drowned
and I had done nothing." Most of us know instinctively what he
means, because sooner or later most people conclude, "I am not
enough for me."

We may be able to survive while some of our fellow Americans drown, but we will not breathe easy. Whenever we look
within ourselves we will be confronted by a glaring discrepancy
between what we are and what we know we could be. As an
individual you can be a success. But only as part of a community
can you be a hero.

The notion of community, of course, applies to our family and
friends, our neighborhoods, our civic associations, our churches
and synagogues. But it applies also to our town, our state, our
region, our country. And one of its highest expressions is the
government that we, as a free people, have established for ourselves. If we've learned anything from our history as a nation, it
is that our government serves as a powerful force for creating,
sustaining, and strengthening the American community.

The Role of Government

All the evidence of the world around us points compellingly to
the conclusion that if we are to grow in strength and civility, we
need to recognize and build upon our relationships to one another and that the most practical way we know to get that done

is through government. The wisdom of helping to bear one another's burdens and to share one another's strengths has been apparent from primitive times, when humans clung together as mates, then families, then clans and tribes. It's where villages, cities, states, and nations came from. The European Community is extending the idea now, taking down old barriers between the nations of Europe; forging an association that is stronger than the sum of its individual parts. And that is just what we did when we abandoned the loose relationship of thirteen states to form a family called the *United* States of America.

Now an anxious, harried America is told that the solution to our problems is to have less government and more individualism, and a serious argument has been started over this fundamental proposition. It deserves a thorough consideration.

When you're a child, how can you tell when you're in big trouble? For me, it was when Momma would enumerate my misdeeds for my father, and finish up by saying to him, "Andrea, I don't know what's wrong with '*tu* figlio'—*your* son." Today, some people talk about our government the same way, as though it were some alien entity, apart from us. If we really want to honor the spirit and achievements of the Founding Fathers, we ought to stop talking about government in the third person and start thinking of it the way it was originally conceived: in the first-person plural. Remember "We the people"? Government is the glove, and we are the hand that moves it. Or in the unforgettable words of Pogo: "We have met the enemy, and he is us!" My mother may have been so furious she couldn't stand to acknowledge me, but I remained very much her responsibility. In the same way, if we don't like today's government, it is up to us to insist it be changed. It is no one's responsibility but our own.

To do justice to that obligation, to make intelligent decisions about when and how we want the government involved and when we don't, we need to agree on some basic ideas of what our government is and what we want it to do for us.

Abraham Lincoln said it best: "The legitimate object of government is to do for a community of people whatever they need to have done, but cannot do at all, or cannot so well do for themselves in their separate and individual capacities." A simple formulation, but a profound one—government is the coming together of people to do for themselves collectively what they could not do individually. That provides a useful test when it comes to assessing the appropriateness of any government function. For convenience, as a working governor, I translated it simply into "All the government we need but only the government we need," and what we need we determine one situation, one issue at a time.

The need for some federal functions is as obvious now as it was to the Framers: for example, the federal responsibility for maintaining the armed forces, securing the borders, and minting a single currency to be used in every state, or the federal obligation to guarantee for each of us the fundamental rights spelled out in the Constitution. It would be absurd to leave it to us as individuals to defend ourselves, or even for the states to do it with fifty state militias. And it works on more modern questions, too, such as the federal duty to allocate finite common resources like the airwaves or to protect against harms that cross state lines like air and water pollution. These are all jobs too big for us as individuals, even too big for the biggest states, and jobs where the need for a uniform national policy makes the federal government the best choice for the task.

Lincoln's definition also helps on questions where Americans haven't always agreed about the need for government action of any kind. Take roads and bridges. If your local highways were too congested, would it make sense for you to get together a group of neighbors, go door to door, and try to raise a few million dollars to add four new lanes to the road? And what if other residents objected to where your group chose to build a new off-ramp? Who would make the final decision—and how? So probably we need the government to build roads and bridges.

What about providing old-age insurance? Should that be solely an individual responsibility? What about the millions whose employers don't provide pensions? How about the people who spent twenty years with a company that went bankrupt before they retired? Doesn't it make more sense to pool our resources, with everyone who works pitching in toward Social Security and drawing from it when they retire?

Should we have state and national parks, or should only those people who can afford a big backyard have access to grass and trees, and only millionaires who own country estates and private beaches have access to their serenity and grandeur? Should government get out of the parks business and just lease the Everglades to Walt Disney and the Grand Canyon to the Marriott Corporation?

What about crime? We could get rid of our three-tiered, local/state/federal system of justice and try private vigilantism—but would that be prudent? Which one of us would volunteer to go up against the Cali cartel? Or what about checking new drugs and food products for safety? Couldn't we just rely on the advertising claims of the pharmaceutical companies? Who needs consumer protection? "Let businesses sell whatever they sell, and if their goods are defective or dangerous and people get sick or hurt or killed, business will dry right up—it's the beauty of the free market. Caveat emptor!" Would any of us really want to live in a world like that?

Should we have speed limits on the highways, or just let each driver decide? If I want to operate a slaughterhouse on the same block as your home, why not? It's my property, isn't it? Should we have deposit insurance for banks and regulators monitoring them for safety and soundness, or should we let just anyone paint "Joe's Bank" on a storefront, and if his customers lose every dime they deposit, that's just their tough luck?

We can also refer to Lincoln in deciding when government—especially the federal government—should keep its hands to itself. Should the government define when or how we worship, by scheduling organized prayer in the public schools? Does the government know better than a woman herself whether she should carry a pregnancy to term? Should the government have a say in determining what may go on in your bedroom between consenting adults? Do you need the government to decide what you should or shouldn't read or see on television?

We may also find that the "right" degree of government involvement in an issue is different at different times. Utilities, for example, have passed back and forth from the public to the private sector over the last century. When the private sector couldn't raise the start-up capital, government did it. When government management grew sluggish, utilities were privatized. When there was inadequate regulation or excessive profits, government intervened more heavily—and in some cases even took back total control.

We've tried some other important things both ways. Take education. In the beginning there was only private education for those lucky enough to get it. We could try that again. No public schools. Parents could take complete responsibility for their children's education. You or your spouse, if you had one, would give up your salary, stay at home, and educate your kids yourself. Of course, you'd have to buy textbooks and supplies, and you'd probably have to take a lot of refresher courses in order to teach your children history and math and science—or stay ahead of them on the computer. Home learning probably isn't practical for most people.

So perhaps you and your neighbors could get together and organize a school. Of course, with no government role in education, and therefore no tax revenues, you'd have to charge hefty tuition, or run a heck of a lot of bake sales or raffles to pay for it. And then there's the question of whether what your school teaches meets the admissions requirements of a good college and the needs of your children's potential employers. How would you handle children with special needs, from the learning disabled to the highly gifted? To resolve these and hundreds of other questions about policies and curriculum, you and your neighbors decide to hire a principal and to elect among yourselves a committee to oversee the school.

By the time you've figured out how to run your new institution, you'll have created, in effect, a form of local government: people coming together to do collectively what they can't do as well or at all by themselves.

Although it's increasingly popular to say that less government is always better, our failure to act together through our government has perpetuated some of our greatest shames as a nation. During our first century, government did little to protect the basic human rights of blacks and women and working people, the sick, the ignorant, the mentally ill, or the old. Were we a better nation without Social Security for the elderly, without civil rights for minorities, without financial aid for college students, without rules regulating pollution?

In assessing the proper scope of government, we ought to remember that government is not just something that helps someone else. Each of us has been helped by government in many ways, yet we tend to take for granted the programs that helped us and to begrudge those that help other people. The New York City straphanger rides the subway to work each day; the suburbanite drives along the expressway. Mass transit and highways—both publicly supported, both government run. One citizen uses food stamps to feed her family, another uses Medicare to pay his hospital bills. One attends a state university, another vacations at a national park, a third gets a home mortgage insured by the FHA (Federal Housing Administration) and a tax deduction for his mortgage interest. If you own property, its value hinges on government investments in the local infrastructure and the wisdom of government zoning regulations.

Of course, it's clear that government is imperfect, sometimes arrogant, sometimes inefficient. Governments—even representative, popularly elected governments—are institutions created and run by fallible humans. "Democracy," Winston Churchill once said, "is the worst system devised by the wit of man, except for all the others." Sometimes government means well but does poorly. Sometimes government makes mistakes. So do businesses; so do military leaders; so do private charities; so do parents. We can all agree on the need to reform welfare, our regulatory process, and much of the rest of what government does, and we'll discuss some of these necessary changes in the next chapter. But government's imperfection is no excuse for going to rash extremes by crippling some of government's vital functions or eliminating them entirely.

Remember when, if you'd just been introduced to someone, you'd find yourselves discussing the weather? Now, in certain circles, the most reliable icebreaker is an anecdote about this or that government stupidity, some wrongheaded decision, some ill-advised regulation. Certainly, sometimes government just plain fouls up. But the current "conservative chic" view extrapolates with dangerous speed from anecdotes into policy, from finding fault with an agency to advocating its abolition. We should try to remember that not every story—no matter how egregious or shocking—has the weight of parable.

Coca-Cola's attempt to market New Coke was a fiasco; if Coca-Cola had been a federal agency, would conservatives have called for its elimination? The Chicago Cubs once traded Lou Brock for Ernie Broglio—one of the biggest mistakes in the history of baseball. Should the Cubs have been disbanded? We've learned of tragic cases of sexual abuse by priests. Does that mean the Catholic Church has outlived its usefulness? The nation's leading fund-raiser for charities—the United Way—was recently embarrassed by a scandal involving misuse of funds and misconduct by top officials. Does that mean charities are bad? There are plenty of dysfunctional families; should we therefore reject "family values"? Our entire private enterprise system virtually collapsed during the Great Depression; should we have given up on capitalism?

In America today, it costs so much to have things repaired that it sometimes seems smarter when an appliance breaks down to throw it out and start again. Unfortunately, today's radical Republicans are treating our government like a toaster that won't pop up anymore. "To heck with it!" they say. "The thing always was a piece of junk." Before we let them heave it out the window, we ought to make a serious effort to fix whatever it is that's broke.

In the end, it's foolish to ask if you're "pro" government or "anti" government. Republicans boasted that their proposal to grant families a $500-per-child tax credit put this question squarely before the public: "Do you think $500 spent by a bureaucrat is better than $500 spent by a parent?" Putting aside the obvious fact that we'd all like to wake up tomorrow with an extra $500 in our pockets, you can't give an intelligent answer without knowing what the government would have done with the money, and without knowing how much you'll lose in government services and benefits that would have to be slashed to pay for the tax credit. When your little girl is sick and you give her cough syrup, aren't you glad that government "bureaucrats" spent some time—yes, and some tax dollars—to ensure the medicine's safety and effectiveness? Isn't that something you as a parent would be hard-pressed to do on your own? And while you might use the tax break to rush out and invest in $500 worth of broccoli, savings bonds, and encyclopedias for your kids, there's nothing to stop your neighbor from "investing" the money in a new set of golf clubs for himself.

Are we always better off taking money out of an investment in order to have more money in our pockets right now? The Republican attitude toward tax cuts is like the shortsighted stockholder who always wants the corporation to pay bigger dividends next quarter, even if the company (and thus, all its shareholders) would be better off in the long run reinvesting the earnings in the business. Or picture a Republican making this case at GM's annual shareholders' meeting: "General Motors has too much money. You should distribute all of your earnings to the shareholders. What's wrong with you guys—do you think $500 spent by a corporate bureaucrat is better than $500 spent by one of your stockholders?"

Attempting to highlight what he describes as his "radically different vision of America," Speaker Newt Gingrich has contended that Democrats believe "the government is the source of all goodness" and "cannot imagine good things being done by the private sector." That's just more political hyperbole. Democrats do not believe either of those two absurd tenets. Goodness stems from many things—including private businesses, families, neighborhoods, churches and synagogues, not to mention the wonders of nature itself. Where we disagree with the Speaker fundamentally is on the question of whether good things can also be done by government—filling in gaps left by the free market and thus strengthening our economy and holding our society together. Newt Gingrich operates as if he sees all virtue in the private sector and none in government. If he practices what he preaches, and if his house ever catches fire, he shouldn't dial 911 or look for a public fire hydrant; he should contact an entrepreneur interested in selling water for profit.

The Federal and State Roles

When we talk about "the government," it sounds like a huge, undifferentiated mass, as if the IRS, the state police, the county jail, and the village garbage truck were all crowded into a single, skyscraping bureaucracy. In fact, of course, we have several tiers of government, each with different strengths. Which raises another question: how do we decide which of them should be responsible for what? How about extending Lincoln's basic formula—that the *federal* government is the *states* coming together to do what they can't do alone, and so on? That's not bad. But the volume and bitterness of the current clamor over states' rights should tell us this subject won't yield easily to simple logic —because to a large extent it is and always has been a question of power.

The Founding Fathers wrote the Constitution, and the states ratified it, expressly to "form a more perfect union" by replacing the feeble and unsuccessful Articles of Confederation. Nevertheless, during the first half of the next century, many argued that any state had the right to nullify a federal law it disapproved of, or even unilaterally to secede altogether. It took a terrible civil war to resolve this issue in favor of a strongly unified nation.

Now, a new wave of politicians wants to turn back the clock in America—to move us backward categorically toward a weak central government, with maximum power vested in the individual states. Congressional leaders talk of devolving programs and responsibilities down to the state level, and the present Supreme Court is reinforcing the trend.

I was governor for twelve years and a state official for eight before that, and I'm a great fan of states and what they can do. But the current notion that handing over a problem to the states or counties or cities leads magically to solving it is foolish. Aladdin's lamps are as rare in Albany or Austin as in Washington. Based on long experience in state government, I can assure you that state officials have to put on their pants one leg at a time each morning, the same as federal officials! And there are some at each level of government who'll get them on backward, no matter how "close they are to the problems of the people."

I agree that all wisdom does not reside in Washington, D.C. But neither does it reside in the state capitals or the town halls. Frankly, it would be hard to explain if it did, since it's America's voters who elect state and local officials—and who also elect national leaders. What's the theory—that we vote wisely in one kind of race but not in the other, or that the fraction of the population that actually votes in most local elections invariably makes better decisions than the rest of us? Many members of Congress and recent Presidents came to Washington only after serving for years in state or local positions. Do they lose their minds when their plane lands at Washington National Airport? Pete Wilson has been a mayor, a U.S. senator, and now a governor. Was he a genius in San Diego, a fool in Washington, and then a wise man again once he arrived in Sacramento? If local is always better, how come the federal Department of Housing and Urban Development has had to take over chaotic and incompetent local public housing authorities like those in Chicago? Why was it that more than twenty states had to turn their children's protective services over to federal control?

This is not to say that the states are "no good." The question again is "Good for what?" In many cases, states may be better equipped to develop programs that respond to local needs, customs, and traditions. And they play an important role as "laboratories of democracy," experimenting with new approaches that are not yet ready for the prime time of national policy.

On the other hand, national standards and national guidelines often make sense. Babies in Mississippi need the polio vaccine just as much as babies in Minnesota. The laws of chemistry and physics that we must teach the next generation of scientists are the same in Pennsylvania as Montana. Your Social Security check or veteran's benefits should neither double nor evaporate if you move from Maine to New Mexico. The wheat or cattle raised in Kansas may be consumed in many other states, so all states have an interest in laws governing the use of pesticides, antibiotics, and growth hormones. And national cooperation isn't a bad idea,

either—unless you really think it makes sense for Oregon to
build a beautiful new highway that stops dead at the border of
California.

Allowing the states to use greater discretion in running federally assisted programs expands opportunities for more intelligent
and creative management. But we need to chart a careful course
lest devolution become an excuse for Washington to cut back its
overall level of support or for the states to abandon a reasonable
level of commitment to nationally recognized standards in areas
like safety and decent living conditions. Those who want to shift
to the states and localities the responsibility for welfare and other
cords in the social safety net are willfully forgetting the lessons
of history. The federal government took on those responsibilities
for the simple reason that the states and cities and rural towns
with the neediest populations lacked the resources to lift their
own people. When you're down, you can't always get back on
your feet without a helping hand. That's why we provide federal
emergency relief when natural disasters strike.

And although no one would contend that returning power to
the states would somehow lead us inexorably back to the age of
slavery, we should remember that the two fiercest battles for
states' rights in our history were, in fact, launched in defense of
a state's right to permit the enslavement of its own people and,
a hundred years later, to segregate them. State and local officials
may know best how to get things done, but that is no guarantee
they will choose to do the right thing in the first place.

It's a question of balance: the federal government should not
trample thoughtlessly over state autonomy. When it hands out
money to the states to support national priorities and goals—
lessening poverty, improving computer literacy, cleaning up wa-
terways—it has a right to decide if the states are spending the
funds fairly and effectively, but it should give them as much
latitude as possible in how they choose to reach those goals. And
it is past time to curb the destructive federal habit of imposing
unfunded mandates on the states—passing laws, setting standards, and instituting mandatory programs without providing the
money to get the job done.

The recent congressional enthusiasm for an unbalanced,

"states'-rights-or-bust" ethic is being fueled by a variety of decisions handed down from our highest court. In a 1995 decision overturning federal legislation that banned guns on school property, the Supreme Court reimposed the kind of limits on federal powers that the nation outgrew sixty years ago. Despite the billions of dollars the federal government spends to improve public schools and to combat crime, despite the undeniable importance of safe and stable schools to the nation's economic well-being, and despite the clear and present danger gun violence poses to young people, the Court concluded that guns in schools was not a fit subject for national legislation under Congress's Commerce Clause power because it was not sufficiently related to interstate commerce.

In another recent case, involving state-imposed term limits on federal officials, the present Court came within one vote of endorsing Justice Clarence Thomas's pronouncement that "The ultimate source of the Constitution's authority is the consent of the people of each individual State, not the consent of the undifferentiated people of the Nation as a whole." As the *New York Times*'s Linda Greenhouse noted, we were one vote away from moving back toward a preconstitutional notion of state sovereignty.

We've tried that before in our nation's history. It didn't work in the late 1700s, when we began as a simple raft of states lashed loosely together by the Articles of Confederation—too loosely, we soon learned, to deal well with problems or opportunities that transcended state lines. It didn't work in the 1800s, when South Carolina and other Southern states championed doctrines of state nullification and secession, and it took Abraham Lincoln and the Civil War to put the nation back together. And it didn't work in the early decades of this century, when the Supreme Court construed congressional powers so narrowly that national efforts to cope with the Great Depression were virtually paralyzed. The notion of every state for itself is even less appropriate for the twenty-first century, when people, commerce, and ideas will traverse state and even national boundaries more readily than ever in our history.

Our growing mobility and interdependence—and our awareness of that interdependence—have made many more of our problems ripe for national attention. Acid rain respects no boundaries; nuclear and other noxious wastes exist everywhere and are transportable. Without national standards on air pollution, companies will locate in states with the loosest pollution controls. Without a national safety net, every state facing a budget crisis will have an extra incentive to cut where it will only hurt the poor.

I believe in a federal government capable of dealing with the concerns of the whole nation, as envisioned first by James Madison, Alexander Hamilton, and John Jay in *The Federalist* papers, and expanded by Andrew Jackson and Lincoln and FDR as the needs of the nation expanded. The biggest, most daunting challenges awaiting us demand national solutions, or at least a national contribution to the solution. Leaving each state to its own devices, transforming us into the Separate States of America, is no solution at all.

Values, Economics, and Government

Of all the speeches I'm ever asked to give, the hardest are graduations. Why? Because it's tough to relax when you feel like a fraud. How dare I, or any member of my generation, presume to give advice to the people who will inherit America from us? Have we done such a great job with this country, or even with our own moral balance sheets, that we're qualified to counsel other people on how to live?

Understand this, however: even if we never deliver a single commencement address, even if we have no children of our own, none of us as adults can duck the job of teaching the next generation what we think they should value. Inevitably, often inadvertently, we teach those lessons all the time: with what we say and don't say, with what we're shocked by and what we accept, with all the things we spend our time and money on—

even with the people we elect and what we expect from our government. The question of how we might actually institute a formal "values curriculum" in the public schools—and whether we ought to—is interesting and complicated. But we often pose it in a way that's naive: "Should we teach our values in the schools?" The point is, we already do; if our schools are silent on the subject of values, we can be sure their silence speaks as eloquently as the most subversive manifesto.

You might never know it from the divisive way "family values" have been debated in the last few years—as though one political faction or the other owns a patent on the concept—but the American people are largely in agreement that we need to reaffirm and reinvigorate our society's values. We want to reanchor America in the basic moral codes that are not only at the core of our own Constitution but are drawn from an even deeper well of wisdom and history—from philosophical, cultural, and religious traditions that stretch back thousands of years. For some, the interest in restoring the old values springs from a vague unease, a creeping sensation that the world used to be a little sweeter; for others, it's already a matter of perfect certainty that calls for strident moments on the soapbox.

Although we may have begun to agree in principle, there's no question we are still likely to differ hotly over what values we value most. Some people talk as though the only things we should really value are a kind of "traditional" bootstrap-lifting, hardworking, just-say-no self-discipline—and a willingness to discipline others. Those values are necessary but not sufficient. Human beings aren't just beasts of burden whose worth is based solely on how steadfastly they can pull a plow. Compassion, tolerance, an ethic of community service and a willingness to help others—the humane values—are equally traditional and equally important to a just and prosperous society.

It's like a parent raising children. You impose rules in your household and enforce them; you try to instill a sense of what we used to call character; you assign your children some chores; you teach them to take responsibility and learn from their mistakes rather than blaming others. But you also hug your kids and praise them when they do well; you comfort them when they are troubled; you try to instill hope and faith in them when they falter. You govern them with love as well as discipline.

We may also disagree about where the collapse of values is most disturbing or destructive. You choose: Which hurts America more? The viciousness and cynicism of our politics? The greed and arrogance that breeds things like insider trading scandals? The false idol of consumerism that litters our landscape with hollow cathedrals called malls and leads us to worship the $130 sneaker? The violence and depravity filling our airwaves and movie screens? Or addiction and illegitimacy in rural shacks and city ghettos? All of these are problems—and despite all our disagreements, we seem to have reached some rough consensus that we ought to do something about them.

What to do is the tricky part—but I believe there's still another question we have to answer first: Why do we think values are important anyway? Isn't this a free society? Doesn't that mean that we can each do what we want and believe what we want, as long as we mind the Constitution and stay out of each other's hair?

The truth is that we need a strong set of shared personal and public values especially because our society is so diverse and free, precisely because we have put our fate in the hands of the free market. We need it to hold us together when competing interests and traditions threaten to pull us apart, and we need it to help us understand who we are as Americans. Because we reject the heavy boot of a police state, we all depend on one another's sense of morality and decency and self-restraint in the struggle to maintain order. And in our free market system, the expression of the cumulative decisions and actions of millions of individuals, individual virtue is indispensable. In large part, our economy rises or falls on the character and conduct of its people —people who either work hard or don't, who are either frugal or wasteful, who are either scrupulous or sloppy, who either treat one another fairly or follow the law of the jungle.

It is this connection between our values, and our freedom and success that makes the question urgent for us now, as we struggle to confront the double-barreled crises of our economy and our social catastrophes. I have made the point that these two problems are inseparably linked, that they cannot be solved independently. To a large extent, those links are made of values, and they connect in a hundred ways.

Just as my parents were able to fight their way out of poverty because of their profound moral strength and their faith in a system of values thousands of years old, a lack of values like hard work, initiative, and self-denial makes it that much more difficult for people to advance themselves economically.

And when a failure of values strikes those at the top—when employees become expenses to cut instead of investments to nurture, when depositors are seen as dupes, when profits and ratings are the only way we measure success—can you really blame the people if it tarnishes their faith in America—and makes them wonder what we should believe in?

The connections go the other way, too. When the doors are closed economically, so that poverty leads to hopelessness, people are naturally more vulnerable to all the corrosive temptations, from violence to drugs. When hardworking parents can't keep pace with the rising cost of living, it snaps the link between effort and reward. When a healthy corporation lays off thousands of breadwinners just to gain a Wall Street reputation for being "lean and mean," families—traditional or not—are destabilized.

At the same time, if our free market is failing to provide enough jobs for people, we are denying them one of the best ways of joining in our common value system—work!—the simple experience of holding a job, cooperating with other people, and earning one's bread with dignity. It's an old idea—and one we have not paid enough attention to in recent years. Sigmund Freud put it very well when he was asked to describe the essential components of mental health: "To love and to work," he said. "No other technique for the conduct of life attaches the individual so firmly to reality as laying emphasis on work; for his work at least gives him a secure place in a portion of reality, in the human community."

Poppa understood this instinctively. I can picture him, standing behind his marble counter in the grocery store, wearing his stained apron. He'd save the ends of the Italian bread and the cold cuts and he'd give these delicious morsels to poor people who would come in the store and ask for food. But first—if they were men—he'd ask them to do a few chores for him—to bring up some cartons from the basement or sweep the front of the store. If they refused, he'd dismiss them. He had no patience for those who expected something—not just something, his cold cuts and bread!—for nothing, those who were not prepared to participate in the community of work.

In saying all this, let me be clear: I don't believe that poverty "causes" crime or immorality any more than affluence "causes" virtue.

But to deny that despair, hopelessness, and lack of opportunity encourage antisocial conduct is as foolish as arguing that because money can't buy happiness, poverty doesn't contribute to unhappiness. One study found that each one percent rise in the unemployment rate correlates with a 3 percent rise in crime, and nearly a 7 percent jump in homicides. In the thirty largest metropolitan areas alone, the increase in joblessness during the recession of the early 1990s was estimated to account for nearly 63,000 additional violent crimes and 224,000 additional property crimes.

It seems clear that if we want to improve our moral condition, we could start by finding ways to find work for more people. But the harshest political arguments of the day ignore this logic. According to the brutal economic determinism the radical Republicans trumpet, if you're poor, it's your own fault. If you're out of work, you're just reaping the bitter harvest of your own flawed character. Sometimes their rhetoric is hard to distinguish from the social Darwinism that justified the robber barons' ruthless brand of capitalism—a philosophy that viewed the attainment of wealth as ipso facto proof of good character, and poverty as proof of shiftlessness—even if the person sunk low in poverty was slaving away for ten hours a day at starvation wages in the very mills and mines that generated the industrialist's riches.

It's helpful to remember just how harsh and prevalent those views were. Take Andrew Mellon, who served as secretary of the treasury under Presidents Harding, Coolidge, and Hoover.

The stock market crash of 1929, the ensuing plunge into the Depression, the millions thrown out of work, the farms foreclosed, the despair and starvation—none of these fazed Mellon. "It will purge the rottenness out of the system," he declared. "High costs of living and high living will come down. People will work harder, live a more moral life. Values will be adjusted and enterprising people will pick up the wrecks from less competent people." Although the diction is quaint, the thought is depressingly contemporary.

I don't doubt that the signers of the Contract would say that I am being too hard on them and overstating their case. "Governor, you know that's not what we think! If you're poor, and trapped in the cycle of welfare dependency, it's not your fault . . . it's the government's!" Senator Gramm, at the vanguard of the New Harshness, epitomizes what I'd call this vampire view of government. To him, government seems to be a fanged creature that sucks the goodness of the people it gets close to. "Government programs established to help out people have changed the way we behave, corrupted our values, diminished our virtue," Gramm declares.

When you give a disadvantaged child an enriched preschool program, are you corrupting the child's values? What value—illiteracy? I suppose if he were a "real" American, he could teach himself to read? When you provide food stamps to a mother trying to feed her family, are you diminishing her virtue? The virtue of bravely watching her children go hungry because she couldn't afford to feed them? When you provide Medicare for the elderly, are you spoiling their sense of stoicism and self-reliance?

Gramm's comments are a classic example of a Straw Men's Wrestling Match: in one corner, "Big Bad Government"; in the other, "Virtue & Morality." In reality, there is no conflict. Government programs aren't inconsistent with good values. Properly constructed and implemented, they can even complement and promote good values. Take President Clinton's family leave legislation, enacted by a Democratic Congress in 1993 over the fervent objections of business lobbyists and their Republican allies. That act of government now makes it possible for parents to spend a few weeks tending to their newborn baby or sick child without risking the loss of their jobs. Is there a value we should encourage more than caring for your own children?

On the other hand, it's not wrong to suggest that government can have a negative impact on society's values. When politicians in Washington pressure corporate lobbyists for campaign contributions and then invite them into the back rooms to help draft legislation, it tells America that money counts more than morality or the merit of your ideas. When government turned a blind eye toward misuse of depositors' funds by the looters of the savings and loans, it made a mockery of responsibility and accountability. When Lyndon Johnson and Robert McNamara lied about Vietnam and Richard Nixon countenanced and covered up the Watergate break-in, they injected America's trusting, optimistic heart with such a caustic dose of cynicism that we still have not recovered totally.

How do we teach the good values instead? The apostles of the New Harshness want to do it through homilies and castigation, lecturing and hectoring, punishments and threats. I say let's do it by example. We should—in our personal lives, through our communities, and yes, acting through our government—teach by doing. Let's demonstrate compassion by offering programs that reach out to those in need. Let's teach responsibility by holding those at the top accountable. Let's not just preach what we say we believe, let's teach it by example, by doing what America needs to regain her momentum forward.

5

Steps on the Way

———

A Southern politician once said, "Any jackass can kick down a barn, but it takes a good man to build one." The point is well taken. It's a lot easier to criticize, but we need to construct: we can't curse our way to a stronger economy and a more civil society.

In the last chapter I offered three ideas that ought to guide us in building our future. First, that to the classic American tradition of individualism we must add the equally American notion of community—the recognition that we are connected to and dependent upon one another, that we are only as strong as our weakest link, and that government both manifests and strengthens our communal bonds. Second, that rather than seeking "smaller" or "bigger" government in the abstract, we should insist on all the government we need but only the government we need—with need determined one issue at a time. And, third, that instead of merely preaching the values and virtues we cherish, we must practice them—expressing and reaffirming them in both our private actions and our public policies.

Now we turn to some of the details that must appear in our specifications for positive change if we are to build the kind of new national community that we need and deserve. These arguments and ideas are not offered as a complete plan of action. That would require thousands of pages of bills and budgets. Rather they are a sampling of some of our toughest problems and a description of how I believe they should be dealt with, following the guideposts and parameters set out in the previous chapter. Once again, I focus on our two primary challenges: finding ways to give our middle-class workers the benefits of our so-called strong economy, and helping to cure our social pathologies.

To find more room in the circle of opportunity for the middle class and those struggling to earn their way into the middle class, we need to use our government to provide more and better education, to invest in research, development, and infrastructure, to promote free and fair trade, and to prune excessive regulation without jeopardizing public health or inviting commercial abuse of consumers. Because the private sector, not government, is the primary engine of growth in our free enterprise system, I suggest we must challenge private employers to view employees as assets at least as important as plants and machinery. Finally, since some Americans will inevitably be left behind in our dynamic, highly competitive economy, government should implement policies that ensure that while not every one will earn the right to dine sumptuously, every American will at least have a place at the table. A particularly important illustration of this governmental safety net role is in the area of health care.

Our approach to the nation's social ills should be premised on the conviction that prevention is preferable to punishment, that inoculating our children with hope works better than combating the aftereffects of despair. This conviction should underlie the approach we take to the vexing challenges of crime, substance abuse, welfare dependency, children having children, and the need to build a society that encourages and teaches positive, life-affirming values.

Finally, any discussion of solutions has to include the federal budget deficit, because we need to be able to make necessary public investments without adding to our nation's terrible burden of debt. At the same time, because the tasks ahead are exquisitely difficult politically and require undivided attention to the public interest, we need structural changes that will allow government to shed the distractions of special interest influence peddling and improve its own efficiency and effectiveness.

It should be clear at the outset that there is no painless way to do all that must be done and that we must work to make progress as fast as we can, because for many Americans the pain is intense and getting worse.

Recognizing what needs changing won't be difficult. You don't have to be an economist or philosopher to know that we need to come to the assistance of workers being squeezed out of their jobs, elderly people who need nursing homes, children threatened by drugs and violence. You don't have to be an educator to know that we can't compete successfully with societies where the school year is sixty days longer than ours. Or a psychologist to know that people who cannot reasonably expect much good out of life may come to settle for what's bad. Nor do you have to be a political scientist to understand that if we don't do a better job of combating inequality, our society will grow increasingly divided and the American Dream will wither on the vine.

To a large extent, the actions I suggest here involve intelligent uses of government applied to some of our major areas of concern. That does not mean, however, that I think government can or ought to be the only lever we use to lift ourselves upward. There are obvious limits to what the public sector can accomplish, just as there are limits to what the private sector can do alone. Building a greater America requires using both.

The Economic Challenge: Restoring the American Dream

A single, simple, four-letter word comes closer to a panacea for our problems than any other I can think of. The word is "work." As Voltaire explained more than two centuries ago, work provides each of us with a precious brand of earthly salvation. It saves us, he wrote, "from three great evils: boredom, vice, and need." There is no heaven until the next life, but for now building an economy with enough work at fair wages for everyone is the closest we can come to a cure for what ails us.

For the most part, today's highly skilled and highly educated workers don't need anybody's help keeping busy and getting paid for it. Our focus should be on the rest of the American family, where older workers are struggling with the fear—or the shock—of layoffs, their younger peers are afraid the skills they worked so hard to gain will be obsolete in half a decade, and those just entering the workforce, with neither skills nor experience to lean on, see a working world that has little room for them.

Nothing in the Contract with America deals significantly with any of these vulnerabilities, and that's unfortunate. In the increasingly competitive battle for the global economy, our left flank is boxed in by the unlimited guerrilla forces of low-wage countries beating us on price, and our right flank risks being overrun by the elite economic cavalry of the few nations that offer quality and innovation competitive with our own. To fight our way out of this hostile valley, we will need to create jobs—and that will mean providing services and making products of exceptional value and selling them to the rest of the world. That, in turn, will take at least five things, all of them attainable by the combined action of government and the private sector: superior education and training; a skilled, motivated workforce; advanced high-tech capacity; first-rate infrastructure; and better access to markets worldwide. It will also require intelligent cooperation between government, business, and labor, especially in terms of regulation and worker development.

The Sine Qua Non: Education

When President Kennedy challenged us to put a man on the moon, he electrified the nation. It reignited all the tough and glorious instincts that had built this country, and made us the world's predominant power: ingenuity, ambition, outrageous nerve, the cowboy spirit. Who else but America had so many of the natural resources for the job?

We need that kind of bold new enterprise now, directed at a different bright goal: the finest schools on earth, an all-out commitment to exceed the rest of the world in the quality of the teaching and training of our young people. Why not? Is there some country richer than we are? Are our children already so well educated we don't need to do more? What logic argues that we should pump billions of dollars more into defense than the Pentagon asks for, and then spite education in the name of austerity? Is there really something else we need to do that's more important—for our spirit or our economy? According to research from the Brookings Institution, between 1929 and 1982, 29 percent of our growth in worker output and 14 percent of our growth in goods and services can actually be credited to gains in education—better schooling for more people.

What we need is not merely a grab bag of aspirations, not just targets to use for reading and math scores, but schools that are the finest in the world. That is a goal we can all embrace, remember, and achieve, because, like the moon shot, this dare is perfect for us. Not only because it offers the satisfaction of achieving something big, but because what will actually be required of workers in the coming century, and what we actually need our students most to master, is exactly what Americans have always been known for—creativity, flexibility, innovation, and adaptability to change. And it is exactly where our competitors are vulnerable.

After World War II, we seized the moment by developing

a whole generation of well-educated, resilient, and disciplined workers with the GI Bill and other incentives. They helped promote a great wave of technological innovation that carried us to dominance in the world markets. In later decades, as we began to lose our fiery ambition and our hunger for excellence, and as low-cost processes and teamwork became the tools of economic advantage, we lost ground to countries whose cultures excelled in those areas. Now, as we enter an age where what's needed as much as high skills is the ability to adapt to change and quickly gain new mastery, America can be in the driver's seat again.

We should not see this challenge as just a game of educational catch-up. Instead it's like one of those exquisite moments on the basketball court when, with the time almost gone and the horn about to sound, you see an opening, you know how to make the play, and you know you were born to make this shot.

But we can't score without shooting.

Since the mid-1970s, the United States has wandered away from the path to better education, higher skills, and higher wages. If we continue to stray, we surely will not have the workforce we'll need to man the economic battle stations in the century ahead. We will have to import even more of our highly skilled employees than the 200,000 permanent and temporary ones permitted each year under current immigration laws. Fortunately, at least on the question of education, we know that we can make a difference in reversing a downward trend. That will take a lot more than money, but it can't be done without making investments either.

We should rely on a few rock-solid basic ideas:

The first step is clear: commitment to serving the community of all our children by expanding and enhancing Head Start. This federally funded program provides an enriched preschool education and social services to low-income children, and it works. Former Head Start participants have lower dropout rates throughout their school careers and lower unemployment rates once they enter the workforce. According to one study, for every dollar we invest in quality preschool programs we gain $2.48 in things like improved productivity and reduced costs for remedial programs; other studies put the figure even higher. Neglecting

Head Start and similar programs in the name of "change" is either incredibly shortsighted or cynical.

Second, we need to make an absolute psychological commitment to our public schools. They are increasingly demoralized by the lurking sense that after what began as a beautiful love affair, America is ready to abandon public education altogether, if she hasn't already. We've known at least since Aristotle that education should be a first priority for government: "The legislator should direct his attention above all to the education of youth." But it was only forty years ago that we offered public schools open to all Americans; surely now is not the time to walk away from that commitment.

Private schools make an immense contribution to this nation's welfare and deserve encouragement as part of our pluralistic system. In my own state of New York, private schools at every level receive generous support in all the areas permitted constitutionally. But New York and the rest of America must acknowledge and respect the primacy of universally available public education, which has helped Americanize and socialize generations of our children. The kind of commitment our public schools need requires that we work toward four goals:

- Smaller classes. Compared to their counterparts at the best private institutions, teachers in our public schools are asked to handle up to twice as many students at a time. Should we be surprised if their results are more uneven? All the studies say the same thing: wherever a school may be, students in smaller classes consistently outperform their large-class peers in math and reading. The small-class strategy has another practical advantage: it's easy both to set objective targets and to measure if they're being met.
- The best possible teachers. Smaller classes will require more teachers, but we also need to attract, develop, and hold on to the best teachers we can. The teachers' unions also need to lead the way by cooperating with intelligent ideas that would make it less cumbersome for new teachers to get certified and would expose existing staff to rigorous ongoing training and evaluation.

- A longer school day and school year. Students from the countries that compete with us economically consistently outperform our children in academic tests. Why? Sometimes we act
as if we believe that there is a special Asian gene for mastering
trigonometry or a German chromosome for excelling in or-
ganic chemistry, but the answer is simpler. In a study done a
few years ago, Japanese and American parents were both
asked this question: "When it comes to success in school,
which matters more, how smart you are or how hard you
work?" Overwhelmingly, the Americans sided with fate, or
how smart you are. The Japanese sided with the human
power of self-improvement. In addition, our competitors also
believe that it's important not only how hard children study
but how long they study. Public school in many Asian and
European countries lasts as long as an adult workday and runs
many days longer every year. While the United States breezes
along with a nineteenth-century 180-day school calendar designed to free up the kids in the summer to work on the family
farm, the Germans send their children to school for 220 days,
the Japanese for 240. Does any mystery linger about why their
children do better on tests? Surely America's famous ingenuity
can figure out the right answer here, even if it costs us the
price of a few B-2 bombers a year.
- Decent school facilities. To a large extent, American public
education is really composed of two systems—an excellent
one that serves the children of the already comfortable and a
wretched one that barely serves the rest. Nothing expresses
the difference more sharply than the difference in the quality
of our schools' physical facilities. Consider this: one-third of
the nation's public elementary and secondary schools need
extensive repair or even replacement of one or more buildings, and almost 60 percent report serious defects in at least
one major system or structural feature like electricity, plumb-
ing, or roofs. In a 1994 survey, the General Accounting Office
recounted shocking examples of substandard school conditions: termites eating not only school library shelves but the
books themselves, raw sewage backed up on school front
lawns, lead paint peeling from classroom walls, light fixtures

so antiquated that burnt-out lightbulbs can't be replaced because no one makes them anymore. Forty-two percent of
schools lack adequate facilities for laboratory science.

The majority of our students are also struggling to prepare
for the twenty-first century in schools that are wired to handle
nothing more sophisticated than film strip projectors. From
wiring to modems to telephone lines, most public schools
lack the systems to make full use of modern computer, video,
or other interactive technologies. And many of the teachers
themselves are ill-equipped to guide their students anywhere
near that famed superhighway of information.

To all these problems, the Republicans provide an answer that
reflects their obsession with individualism. They want education
"vouchers" to give more parents the "choice" of where their
children attend school, even using public dollars to pay private
school tuition. Giving parents and children the right to choose
schools within the public school system is a good idea. By forcing schools within each district to compete with each other for
students, choice can improve quality and variety in public education. Even so, it is not without its complications: the system must
be designed so that it increases educational opportunity for *all*
children, not just those with highly motivated parents or easy
access to private transportation. We must also make sure that
choice does not lead to schools segregated by race or class.

I fought hard for the principle of public school choice in New
York State, and our successes became models for the nation. But
I'm convinced for a number of reasons that we should resist the
growing pressure to extend choice to private institutions as well.
It's simply not an even competition: private schools would
quickly cream away a small fraction of the most talented students, while leaving behind the vast majority—among them the
most troubled and disadvantaged—and leaving the public
schools with less money than ever to help them. America should
make a better choice—let's choose to invest in our children and
our future by ensuring that *all* of our public schools provide
a decent, safe, and technologically up-to-date environment for
learning.

Third and finally, we have to face the fact that for those who do not go on to four years of college—70 percent of our students—high school is the best and perhaps the only chance they have to prepare for the working world, and in that respect high school for the most part is letting them down. As springboards go, even a good high school education is not very springy, and it's likely to land its owner unceremoniously and forever in the shallow end of the economic pool. We must do better at helping the non-college-bound make the transition to work, equipping them with skills for good-paying jobs as cooks, mechanics, computer technicians, carpenters, and the like.

Part of the answer is to bring businesspeople into our schools and students into the workplace, before they're actually under pressure to bring home a paycheck. There are plenty of ways to do it, and we should pursue all of them, from working with local companies to set up internships, apprenticeships, and cooperative learning programs on a grand scale, to changing what we teach in the classrooms to make it more directly relevant to the world of work. The emphasis should be not only on academic fundamentals but also on the skills, work habits, and attitudes it takes to hold any job at all. All these things are part of New York's highly successful version of this idea called Career Pathways.

With efforts like these, we can bring young people into the race with a running start. Harder to know is how to help workers further down the track, those who find that fate has reached out and tripped them in the stretch: all of a sudden no job, too old, all the wrong skills, perhaps even an industry that has disappeared altogether.

On paper, the solution looks easy and like a perfect place for government action: "Hey, once we get those people into the unemployment office, we can just channel them into public programs that will retrain them for the high-skill jobs of the future!" Unfortunately, it turns out that government isn't very good at the retraining game, in part because it's hard to forecast the needs of employers for set numbers of workers with particular skills and in part because the best place to learn a job is on the job, not in a training center. To give unemployed workers a menu of options wider than government can provide, we need to explore ideas like vouchers that would allow the private sector to do the job training it is so well suited for. Another good idea—if Congress insists on tax cuts—is to use President Clinton's plan to allow tax deductions for college education and job training expenses, in contrast to the Republican plan, which subsidizes investment in capital goods like machinery but not investment in people. And surely there's a role here for the unions, who understand so well their members' strengths and vulnerabilities. A two-way commitment to ongoing training can be negotiated as part of any package a union accepts.

Republicans tell us it is too expensive to train and educate our people, even as they argue that we should give billions of dollars more than the Pentagon asks for defense. Governing is largely a matter of choices. For our nation's sake, we should choose education. The one thing we can't afford to do in preparing our people is too little or nothing, which is all the Republicans offer.

As we look down the road, a few key demographic trends suggest that the whole question of job growth, training, and retraining will grow harder before it grows easier. With every year that goes by, America's workforce becomes increasingly nonwhite and increasingly female, meaning that more and more of our workers will be drawn from two groups that have traditionally come to the workforce with less preparation and fewer skills and found it tougher to make real headway over time.

Which brings us to the subject of affirmative action.

Mend It, Don't End It

If more and more of our workforce will be black, Hispanic, and female, then business, out of self-interest alone, needs to find ways to bring those workers into the workplace more smoothly and develop their strengths so there will actually be enough highly skilled people available to be hired. Over the last six decades, we've used a number of tools, from unemployment insurance to college loans, to even out the ruts and ridges in the open field of American opportunity. On the whole, these instruments have been accepted and even applauded by most people. But one of them, affirmative action, has recently become a national flash point for everything that is still explosive about our race relations and class resentments.

Though the issue is as incendiary as a Molotov cocktail, it has been chucked around recklessly as a political football, just as school busing and scatter-site affordable housing were back in the early 1970s. At that time, in discussing those difficult issues, I urged that we look for less frightening and divisive ways to achieve the worthy goals of those programs, and I believe that's what we need to do for affirmative action today.

We have to ask ourselves a number of questions about affirmative action in all its manifestations, from government contracting to corporate hiring to college admissions. Has affirmative action helped advance talented people whose gifts would otherwise have been neglected? That seems certain. Has the principle been applied unfairly in some instances and left a trail of resentment in others? Again, that seems clear. Do those abuses and unpleasant side effects mean that the concept has outlived its usefulness? Not, I believe, if you see the same America I do.

No one would argue that America has put behind her completely the prejudices, social inequalities, and ugly habits of the heart that made affirmative action necessary in the first place. To start with, blacks, for example, are still unemployed at twice the rate of whites, just as they were in 1960. Women are still paid substantially less than men and are still virtual strangers in many of our hierarchies of power.

Even on that basis, does it make sense to give someone a job because of his or her race or sex? Of course not, no more sense than it would to deny someone a job on that basis. On the other hand, does it make sense when considering two strong candidates for one position, to give some weight to the fact that one belongs to a group traditionally excluded? Yes, as I did during my twelve years as governor, when I appointed to New York's highest court seven white men—and the first two African-

Americans to serve full terms, the first Hispanic, and the first two women, including the first female chief judge.

Two other considerations should guide our assessment of the current controversy. First, we should stop making a fetish out of the unrealistic notion that there is some reliable way to make hiring decisions strictly on the basis of a precise ranking of qualification or merit. Test scores are limited in their predictive value, interviews are subjective, and prior experience is not always an unmitigated plus. Second, we should concede the real value of diversity in our classrooms and work sites. In many settings, diversity is not merely a virtue but a virtual necessity; for instance, how can a police force in a city with a large Hispanic population do its job properly without Spanish-speaking officers?

Surely, as the debate over affirmative action persists, we should correct immediately any cases where our policies are ambiguous, excessive, or simply in error, both to protect individuals of every background and to preserve the credibility of the very concept of affirmative action. As President Clinton and others have suggested, we should look at whether it makes sense to extend the same kind of affirmative, inclusive policies to people struggling to make their way past the handicap of poverty.

We should remind each other that quotas have been illegal for years and are no one's idea of a solution. And at the same time, we should lead America back to the great original goal of affirmative action: to make an extra effort, in seeking and developing talent, to look beyond our familar contacts and networks and well-worn paths, to go outside the small circle of people who look or talk or act just like us and reach out to capable human beings from groups we foolishly excluded in the past.

Helping Business Grow

We can all agree that the free enterprise system is the rich orchard that sustains the American way of life. If you believe today's radical Republicans, however, government is the maniac who charges in with a screaming chain saw of taxes and regulations, leaving nothing but stumps in the wake of his "harvest." The truth is, of course, that government is as essential to our economy as the farmer is to the orchard. Certainly government can and sometimes has interfered excessively or foolishly. But without rules to govern the market, free enterprise becomes a vicious free-for-all. And there are many positive things we can do for business, through our government, that business simply cannot do alone. Today, in at least three areas, we actually need government to do much more for business than just get off its back.

High tech is the first concern: the best single source for the next generation of high-wage American jobs. How can government help? By helping business find a way around the prohibitive costs of high-tech research, the risks of starting new companies, and the economically awkward aftermath of the Cold War.

The growth of our economy for much of the last forty years has been steadily fueled by the results of high-tech research, but the scientific work itself is now increasingly complex and expensive. Not every industrial park can have its own particle accelerator, so it's in the interests of the larger community to pool our resources. Why not make the most of the fact that government already funds a lot of this kind of research through colleges and universities? To stoke our economic growth, we need to turn new discoveries into new products and processes as fast as possible, and the best way is to have businesses and university researchers working together from the start. In New York, as in some other states, we set up a number of public/private partnerships, called Centers for Advanced Technology (CATs), in cutting-edge fields like biotechnology, telecommunications, advanced ceramics, multimedia, and computers. Those CATs have been steadily spinning off new patents and even companies ever since. In that same spirit, we need more, not less, federal support for research and development with commercial applications.

Government can also make a big difference for new high-tech firms just getting on their feet. New businesses ordinarily have extremely high mortality rates; most of them die within the first five years. But you can improve that rate substantially if you can help them cut unnecessary costs. Once again, the answer is pooling resources for the greater good. If you have ten tiny high-tech start-ups, should each of them have its own receptionist? Its own copy machine? Its own "clean room"? Why not pull them all into a single headquarters where they can share all that overhead, and concentrate on building their businesses and creating new jobs? State-sponsored business incubators like these are already working in New York; we should expand the concept and look for other intelligent, job-spawning ways to pool our strength.

Government has a special role to play in repairing the economic havoc that was the unintended side effect of winning the Cold War. For nearly 2 percent of the U.S. workforce, the Cold War ended, or soon will, at a cliff called unemployment. By 1998, as many as 2.6 million Americans may have been pushed over the edge, often losing not just jobs but the kind of well-paid, high-skill jobs our economic growth depends on. We can watch the plunge and call an ambulance, more or less the equivalent of writing unemployment checks. Or we can, wherever possible, intervene before the layoffs start to help defense contractors diversify, make the switch into commercial production, and master the commonplace mysteries of things these giant government contractors never had to think about before, like analyzing market needs and advertising themselves.

Conservatives will invariably denounce these moves as "industrial policy": "Government shouldn't be picking winners and losers! Let the market decide." But let's not kid ourselves: much of our current defense spending has become a de facto national industrial strategy, only without being particularly strategic. Decisions over closing surplus military bases or producing new generations of weapons have become struggles for local jobs and community development. The same members of Congress who would resist with all their might federal spending on high-speed railroads or inner-city housing, fight with all their strength to save defense jobs in their districts. They argue the "strategic" need for an air force base located in their community or for a submarine or bomber produced by a company based in their state, when their real concerns are economic. The job-saving instinct is commendable . . . but if we're going to spend additional billions on public projects, why not channel our limited federal resources into activities that not only save jobs now but also constitute investments that can become the foundation for a strong U.S. economy in the century ahead?

Finally, we can assist businesses in ways that lead directly to jobs—business assistance that trickles up, not down. We can extend targeted jobs tax credits that provide a federal tax incentive for employers to hire and train entry-level workers from disadvantaged groups; establish enterprise zones in which a package of federal, state, and local inducements are offered to businesses that invest and create jobs in economically distressed areas; and provide loan guarantees or low-interest loans to small businesses seeking to expand.

Infrastructure

Beyond these high-tech steps, the second place we need to do more to help business is with respect to the unromantic but indispensable subject of infrastructure. We inevitably take it all for granted, the highways and train tracks, the airports and harbors, the dams and water supply systems that none of us would do without and none of us could do alone. The Republicans' Contract doesn't even mention it, and their budget proposes real infrastructure cuts, especially in Amtrak and mass transit. But make no mistake: our infrastructure is the backbone of our economy. No nation can retain its posture as an economic leader if its spine is collapsing.

From nineteenth-century "internal improvements" like the Erie Canal to Eisenhower's interstate highway system, the road to America's economic dominance has been paved with generous investments in the common infrastructure that transports our goods and people and harnesses our natural resources. Do we have similar needs and opportunities today? Yes. Are we neglecting them? Yes. Will we come to regret it? Yes, unless we do something about it soon.

On the whole, our infrastructure may seem fine, but by some estimates, 40 percent of our roads and bridges aren't even up to par. Where our infrastructure is currently inadequate, it costs us money, and where we're failing to make proper investments for the future, it will cost us opportunity. For example, in urban areas where there is too much car and truck traffic for the infrastructure to handle, highway congestion already costs America more than $30 billion a year in lost productivity and wasted fuel.

Should we just live with the waste and aggravation, and allow deterioration to become disaster, or does it make sense to invest in public transportation and "smart" highways that can virtually eliminate the lineups at toll booths and direct drivers to less-congested routes? Our international competitors are investing billions in things like high-speed rail, fiber optic communications, and facilities like harbors and airports that encourage trade and tourism, while we, trapped by the Republicans' simplistic antigovernment mantra, are allowing our existing infrastructure to sink in many places toward disarray and obsolescence. Frugal? Or penny wise and pound foolish?

In some cases, we need to focus on direct government investment and control. The Queensborough Public Library opened the world of books to poor and middle-class immigrant kids growing up in my old neighborhood in South Jamaica, Queens. The Tennessee Valley Authority brought electricity to the mid-South in the 1930s. Public service commissions made sure that rural areas were wired for telephone service, whether or not it seemed economically appealing to the phone company. In the same way, it will take both direct government investment and thoughtful regulation to make sure that everyone in our society has at least minimal access to computer technology and advanced telecommunications.

In other instances, government may only need to help orchestrate or jump-start the financing, as with harbor front revitalizations where developers are only too eager to be the main players.

Infrastructure investments have such obvious benefits to all of us as a community that it's hard to understand how the Republicans miss the point. An advanced and well-kept infrastructure represents not only a foundation for and stimulus to private development and growth, but a terrific source of new jobs on its own, in fields like construction and engineering. In fact, it may also offer one of the clearest ways to rescue displaced workers and move people off welfare and into real private sector jobs: matching them with companies that have contracts to build, repair, or operate public infrastructure facilities.

Trade

If our goal is to create more good jobs here in America, we need to take even more aggressive steps to encourage exports by breaking down trade barriers in other nations and pursuing foreign contracts and opportunities for American firms. In particular, we should focus on the so-called emerging markets in Asia, Eastern Europe, and Latin America, since that's where two-thirds of the world's economic growth will occur over the next two decades. America stands to do especially well in those markets in fields like energy, telecommunications, insurance, transportation, and environmental and medical products and services.

While we're busy knocking out the barriers to free trade wherever we can, we should keep two principles in mind. First, that we want to succeed in the international economic competition by promoting rising living standards, more humane labor laws, and stronger environmental requirements in other countries, not by agreeing to compromise our own standards on these questions here at home. The second principle is that although it may be disconcerting philosophically to have American firms owned by foreigners, direct foreign investment in the United States can be desirable, as long as it produces jobs for Americans, and unless and until foreign interests are in danger of having too much control. We are nowhere near that point.

There's something else that helps us create American jobs and that is our Department of Commerce. In the Republicans' drive to dissolve at least one major government agency, they have set their sights on Commerce—a puzzling choice for pro-business politicians, since the Department of Commerce is both a strong force for promoting U.S. exports and a constant day-to-day help to the nation's small businesses. Closing it would be another bad deal offered by the Contract with America.

The Thickets of Regulation

There are other important ways we can use our government to encourage the growth of jobs and business in general, but few are as popular as the idea of cutting back on regulation. Even tax cuts appear to take second place on the Republican business agenda.

Why? Two reasons, I think. First and obviously, almost by definition regulation costs business money, both because of the steps business must take to comply with a rule, like putting scrubbers in its smokestacks or giving workers safety training, and because of the paperwork it sometimes takes to document compliance. For people who make a living trying to keep their costs low, any extra cost is inherently irritating, especially if it doesn't seem to be achieving anything worthwhile. Which brings us to the second motive for the outcry against regulation. In the last few decades, some agencies that regulate business seem to have lost their sense of proportion, letting rule after rigid rule pile up, leaving many businesses feeling legitimately injured or harassed. The Democrats largely ignored the syndrome when they held the power and appear sheepish about dealing with the need for change now. The new Republican conservatives predictably lurch too far in the other direction. Instead of accepting the clear need for some basic monitoring and working to eliminate excessive regulation, they suggest steps that would, in effect, wipe out some of our most essential protections.

It's as if the Republicans not only want to throw the baby out with the bathwater, they want to make sure we never have a baby or run a bath again. One example: a favorite Republican target is OSHA, the Occupational Safety and Health Administration begun in 1970 to enforce rules governing decent working conditions. In the intervening years, the rules and regulations that OSHA developed have in some cases grown so complex and detailed as to be almost unenforceable, and it appears that some OSHA inspectors have made things worse by taking an absolute "the-rules-is-the-rules" approach. But for all OSHA's flaws, in the twenty-five years of its existence the agency has saved the lives of an estimated 140,000 American workers and cut job-related fatalities by half, and each year it prevents 100,000 workplace injuries, according to Public Citizen's Congress Watch. Can't we work something out here? Isn't it smarter here —as in other places—to mend it but not end it?

Republicans are rigid in their stance because they know that their rhetoric resonates with many Americans. Resistance to being told what to do is intrinsic to the American character. We were born breaking rules—Great Britain's rules. Show an American a speed limit and he'll exceed it. It's part of our impulse for freedom and the pursuit of American happiness. Nothing wrong with that impulse—until it's taken too far and endangers others. What we need here, as in so many other situations, is a little more subtlety. We're not teenagers who swear we would rather die than follow our parents' rules. Or we shouldn't be. Maturity recognizes the intelligence and wisdom that lie between the extremes.

Modern-day conservatives talk as if government restriction of property or business rights in the public interest is some sort of wild-eyed notion foisted on them by contemporary liberalism. Actually, it is one of the oldest notions in our common law traditions. The maxim *Sic utera tuo ut alienum non laedas*— utilize your property in such manner as to not injure that of another—dates as far back as twelfth-century England, and became a crucial part of the British common law tradition that the

United States adopted from the start. As the great jurist Oliver Wendell Holmes put it in the nineteenth century:

> The government may, by general regulations, interdict such uses of property as would create nuisances, and become dangerous to lives, or health, or peace, or comfort of the citizens . . . on the general or rational principle, that every person ought so to use his property as not to injure his neighbors, and that private interests must be made subservient to the general interests of the community.

Holmes understood that no matter how inconvenient regulation might be to an individual or business, if the rules were properly designed, they would serve the interest of the whole community in terms of safety, quality of life, and sometimes sheer economics.

You could surely build buildings more cheaply if there were no building and fire codes, but once you factored in the loss of human life and property from fires or building collapses, it wouldn't be sound economics. According to a National Highway Traffic Safety Administration study, federal auto and traffic safety actions taken between 1966 and 1990, like imposing crashworthiness standards on vehicles, have saved 243,000 lives, with a net economic benefit to society of $410 billion. The total lack of regulation in the securities industry before 1929 surely contributed to the infamous stock market crash that launched the Great Depression. And what about the savings and loans in the 1980s, which collapsed after they were deregulated? Today, the stock market and the banking industry are highly regulated, and America can boast of one of the richest and strongest capital markets in the world.

The truth is, sometimes regulation proves useful for society and for business. If we had no laws governing pollution from smokestacks, a factory that spent extra money installing antipollution equipment might well be less profitable than others that kept on happily polluting away. But since we all benefit from cleaner air, we impose emissions standards that every factory has to meet. That way, every company bears only its fair share of the expense.

And sometimes the benefits to business are even more obvious. When the government set fuel-efficiency standards for cars, Detroit kicked and screamed. But the government rules turned out to be a blessing in disguise. By forcing the Big Three automakers to develop fuel-efficient cars, the rules actually helped the domestic auto industry compete against increasingly popular fuel-efficient imports. In the same way, air bags, an idea imposed by government, are now a key feature in marketing new cars.

What makes some degree of regulation both necessary and wise is the undeniable fact of our interconnectedness as a community, and there's no better example than the question of environmental policy. We say "no man is an island," and in the case of the environment that's true in a palpable way.

Moreover, the very value of private property is not determined as though each plot of land were an island. The value of a plot of land is safeguarded by government zoning that prohibits noxious uses in adjacent plots and enhanced by government-built roads and sewers and public schools. A house in a district with excellent public schools can easily be worth $50,000 more than the identical house in a nearby district with inadequate public schools.

What each of us does on our land directly affects others: our neighbors most immediately, but not alone. Pollution travels through the air, through the earth, through the water. Poisons generated in one place travel with the wind to taint other regions, as they did after Chernobyl. A developer who builds in a floodplain raises the risk of flooding in the surrounding area as well.

But it's not as if we have to sit by passively and watch those interconnections work to our disadvantage. New York recently demonstrated a way to achieve environmental goals through flexible regulatory approaches that factor in the needs of the businesses in question. Discovering that New York City's water supply was being tainted by agricultural runoff from upstate New York farms, the city's initial response was a truckload of regulations that would have imposed unworkable limits on the farmers and in some cases even forced them to shut down. This traditional top-down strategy was predictably divisive. Fortunately, wiser heads prevailed: farmers' representatives began negotiating with city officials, and they jointly developed a cooperative program. Now, New York City will help pay for upstate farm improvements—designed by the farmers—that reduce contamination at the source without crippling farm operations, and save the city the immense cost of a major new water filtration plant.

In an era preoccupied with restoring strong values, it's worth noting that reasonable regulation of the environment is not only practically useful, it is a moral imperative. Commitment to preserving the ecological balance comes as close to a purely selfless concern as we get in politics. Our generation could do quite well, perhaps, by consuming environmental resources without limit—felling as much timber as our chain saws can cut, catching all the fish with no concern for preserving their spawning patterns, disposing of waste in whatever way seems cheapest and most convenient. But we institute measures to save the earth for the benefit of generations to come: people we will never know and who will never know us.

That kind of care for something larger than oneself is the ultimate basic value, and for many of us that consoling truth is enough to justify whatever current inconveniences regulations may create. But as I've noted already, there are other pragmatic reasons for resisting the sworn enemies of regulation. In areas like consumer protection, antitrust, health and safety, and the environment, a reasonable level of regulation helps the marketplace function more efficiently, promotes a level playing field, and ensures that people and firms are treated fairly by the government. Like rules in sports, regulations promote healthy competition. Boxing without rules would be mayhem. So would business. Indeed, for a while it was.

The point has been made many times, but never better than in Robert Bolt's play *A Man for All Seasons,* about Thomas More, a lawyer and lord chancellor of England, the man ultimately responsible for the everyday administration of justice in the courts and chanceries of King Henry VIII. In the play as in real life, More faced the temptation to step outside the law, to disregard the law's protections and distinctions, to accomplish goals quickly and cleanly, even if the route was technically illegal. He refused the temptation.

He talked one day with his son-in-law, William Roper, who mocked More's insistence on abiding "the thickets of the law" and suggested that if necessary he, Roper, would cut down the whole forest of legal technicalities to get at the devil.

In the play, More answers him: "Oh? And when the last law was down, and the Devil turned round on *you*—where would you hide, Roper, the laws all being flat? This country's planted thick with laws from coast to coast—man's laws, not God's— and if you cut them down . . . d'you really think you could stand upright in the winds that would blow then? Yes, I'd give the Devil benefits of law, for my own safety's sake."

Pruning back overly rigid, outmoded regulations is an ongoing process that is part of good government, and the Democrats should be engaged in that process, but all of us should reject calls to hack indiscriminately at regulation in order to clear shortcuts to the goals of the moment. The rule of law, no matter how inconvenient, is what holds us together as a civilized community of people.

The Challenge for the Private Sector

If these are the tasks for our left hand, called government, what can the right hand of private enterprise do to bolster the economy and reinforce the strength of our community? Republicans argue that we should do nothing but let the free market be free, and we certainly can all agree that the key for business is to stick to the knitting of the cozy old-fashioned sweater of profitability. But it's worth understanding that the sweater can be made equally well in different patterns, and some of them are a much better fit with the interests of our national community.

We have to start with the understanding that it's not a good idea for the United States to try to win the low-wage race to economic victory, even if individual companies can score by exporting their jobs overseas. The only race worth our running is the one for higher quality—and winning it will require having the best workers in the world. Here are some of the next steps American business could make to move the country in that direction, for the good of us all:

- Business could make a much more serious commitment to training and retraining. Only 12 percent of all workers in the United States have the benefit of job training through their employers, while in the countries we compete with participation rates are two to three times as high. German employers also spend 2.4 times more per worker on training than American firms do. Why? Because they know it's a good idea economically. Workers whose employers provide formal on-the-job training tend to be paid more down the line, but they also tend to become more productive, and their gains in productivity more than offset the rise in what they're paid. It's a win-win situation.
- Companies could resist the temptation to cut too deeply into staff. After the frenetic swirl of layoffs in the last few years, some corporations have starved themselves of human resources to the point of diminishing returns. Although payroll slashing generally follows pressure from shareholders and the stock market for higher profits, it's far from certain to produce a positive financial outcome. One study revealed that of companies who went on a radical diet of downsizing, less than half reported a rise in earnings, and only 34 percent a rise in productivity. Frankly, it shouldn't surprise anyone: when employees vanish in large numbers, the sum of their expertise disappears with them. And could any of us concentrate effectively on work, whether in an assembly line or an office, knowing that the folks on either side of us just lost their jobs?
- Corporations could work actively with labor toward a sense of cooperative venture and shared risk. That means bringing employees into the process of corporate decision making and giving them more of a stake in efficiency and innovation through arrangements like profit sharing. In our national battle for more good jobs, organized labor also has a heavy responsibility to discard adversarial antimanagement strategies, develop more flexible approaches, and help employees

understand how their fates are linked to the company's profitability and how their actions can affect it. As too many unions have already found out, there is no honor in self-imposed obsolescence. Of course, labor unions can't do enough to foster a productive, competitive workforce if they represent a dwindling percentage of workers (one out of ten in the private sector). Unions need to revitalize themselves with new members, new leaders, and new tactics in order to reclaim their historic role in promoting decent wages and working conditions for average Americans.

Some corporations and unions have adopted progressive strategies like these but most still lag behind. Government shouldn't try to compel these choices; it can, however, encourage them with incentives. For example, the pressure that pushes companies into layoffs often comes from big institutional investors, like pension fund managers, who control hundreds of thousands of shares and expect to be heard when they ask for higher returns. Some of these major investors have started to take a broader view of their responsibility to the larger community. California's public employee pension fund, which controls $80 billion in assets, recently announced it would start giving consideration to the employment practices of the companies in its portfolio.

Why shouldn't government make the same kind of assessment when corporations come looking for tax breaks, subsidies, regulatory relief, or procurement contracts? Let's make sure that when government helps business, it's helping the employees as well as the employers. As we do when we seek to influence personal conduct, we should consider a carrot-and-stick approach to influence corporate conduct. Government could offer lower taxes or other preferential treatment to companies that pay decent wages and benefits, that share productivity gains with their workers, and that provide a reasonable degree of job security. Conversely, government could restrict tax deductions or other public largesse to companies whose routes to higher profits are paved at the expense of lower living standards for their workers. And why shouldn't we require corporations to include in their annual reports an assessment of the impact of layoffs on their workers and communities? That might focus attention on the true social costs of downsizing.

When People Slip Off the Ladder

The preceding sections of this chapter have described ideas to help people obtain employable skills and to help business create jobs. But even if business and government did all the right things, from training workers to promoting exports, from improving schools to modernizing infrastructure, our economy for the foreseeable future will leave some Americans behind. In an age defined by fast-paced technological change and intense global competition, many Americans can expect to lose their jobs to automation or to overseas factories. Despite our best efforts, many will still find themselves slipping off the bottom of the economic ladder into a free fall of declining wages, evaporating benefits, and temporary work. Both common sense and compassion argue for us to try to catch these Americans and their families before they plunge into despair or succumb to the undertow of our social pathologies.

A dynamic, high-tech, globalized economy may produce greater riches for all of us in the long run, but that is not much comfort right now to the assembly-line worker laid off because his company moved its plant abroad or the telephone operator who was automated right out of her job. Speaker Gingrich paints a rosy portrait of the Third Wave economy of the twenty-first century, but these people need to find a way to put food on their dinner tables in 1996, 1997, 1998, and 1999.

In addition to all we do to help the economy grow, we also need to take steps to assist those who are hurting now. If we understand "community" not so much as a nice idea but as a necessary one, we can see why it makes sense to make room at the table for every American. The marketplace can be harsh; capitalism works because it has losers. But surely in modern America, losing in the unforgiving competition of the free market shouldn't mean losing one's dignity as a human being or one's ability to obtain life's necessities. The community of America is only as strong as its weakest link. We must strengthen all the links in our chain so that all Americans can keep pulling together.

For the last sixty years in this country, we have generally agreed that government should play a key role in cushioning those in vulnerable circumstances from the merciless indifference of the free market. Although today's Republicans claim otherwise, the goal is not to punish the successful for their success nor to establish a Utopia through social engineering. The goal is to relieve the palpable suffering of human beings who are taking a beating. There are two means of doing it, and both are useful: we can find ways to get more cash into the hands of the poor, and we can make specific facilities and services available for the entire community, including the poor, so that their lack of cash matters a bit less.

The first focus is to increase people's spending power, and one of the best techniques is to make sure they are paid fairly for their work. We can raise the minimum wage, enforce laws against unfair labor practices so workers and unions have the leverage to bargain for reasonable wages, and encourage profit sharing and employee ownership plans so workers benefit from their own rising productivity. We can close the loophole in our immigration laws that permits U.S. firms to replace their permanent employees with temporary foreign "guest workers" at lower wages. The Republicans portray steps like these as unacceptable meddling in the workings of the free market; I believe they are inescapable responsibilities in the interests of national community.

We also have a variety of more direct governmental programs to give struggling people access to a little more cash. Not surprisingly, the signers of the Contract are suspicious of all of them. For those laid low by unemployment, we offer unemployment benefits; for those with disabilities, Supplemental Security Income; for the working poor, the Earned Income Tax Credit. The Republicans are looking hungrily at all three as deliciously easy places to cut, as soon as they're done with Aid to Families with

Dependent Children. It should concern us all that the people who would be hurt have practically no voice politically.

What's more, under the banner of simplicity, many of today's congressional Republicans are backing away from our tradition of taxing people progressively, that is, according to their ability to pay. Unfortunately, the "flat tax" reform they advocate would actually make our already troubling income inequality even worse. Apparently it makes sense to today's conservatives that of every $1,000 you earn, you should pay the same percentage to the government whether you're washing dishes in a swanky restaurant, you own the place, or the best table is always reserved in your name. Another variation that would similarly widen the already dangerous gap between haves and have-nots is replacing the progressive income tax with a consumption tax. Either of these "reforms" would be such a boon for the affluent, they will think Christmas falls on April 15. The last thing our government should be doing is shifting more of the tax burden onto those struggling to maintain their precarious foothold on the ladder of economic opportunity.

The second role for government is to counteract the effects of inequality by strengthening the pillars of our public life. A corporate CEO may earn $1 million a year while his secretary earns $35,000 and the janitor who cleans the corporate headquarters at night is lucky to bring home $200 a week. Americans don't begrudge the corporate chieftain his fine home, his luxury cars, his yacht, his first-class travel, his kids' access to the most prestigious private schools. He can afford a lot of things the secretary and the janitor can't. But shouldn't the secretary and the janitor be able to count on health care when they're sick? Shouldn't their children have decent public schools to attend? Shouldn't their families have national and state parks for recreation? Aren't all the people who work for that company part of the family of America? Doesn't government have an interest in ensuring that all Americans have basic necessities and are provided with quality public services?

Or look at it this way: the free enterprise system gives people with money access to an almost unlimited variety of books through commercial bookstores, but there's also room in America for public libraries, where access to knowledge is not constrained by ability to pay. Bookstores are wonderful . . . but so are public libraries. In this as in so many questions, a vibrant private sector augmented by an enlightened government produces the best answer.

With that principle in mind, we need to work together, through our government, to make sure that every American, both the $6-an-hour retail clerk and the $300-an-hour lawyer, has access to a basic complement of facilities and services: schools, health care, libraries, parks, cultural facilities, transit, child care, youth recreation programs. When we strengthen these public assets, we provide the underpinnings of a decent life even for those trapped by low wages or dislocated by economic change. And that still leaves people plenty of incentive to improve their circumstances through their own hard work.

Curing Our Ailing Health System

On both economic and moral grounds, it is inexcusable that our great nation has not assured all our citizens adequate, affordable health care. Accounting for one-seventh of our economy, our health care system can help us thrive or can, when it's out of whack, impose awful burdens on households, businesses, and government. Morally speaking, the issue is just as clear. As I told the New York State Legislature in my 1993 Special Message on Health Care System Reform:

> [W]e face a system of paradoxes and contradictions. Our health care system is capable of breathtaking technological breakthroughs, and we have the finest physicians and medical facilities in the world. But millions of Americans find that adequate care is out of reach. We can perform therapeutic miracles, but we have not found ways to provide basic health care for all who need it. . . . [W]orld-renowned centers of excellence are within blocks of communities with health indicators and standards of care typical of underdeveloped countries on distant shores.

Our nation has already taken the first bold step in applying the idea of community to health care. At first, it was controversial, opposed by both the medical establishment and the political predecessors of today's Republicans. But today it is considered an indispensable element of the social contract, an entitlement in the moral as well as legal sense. That program, of course, is Medicare, which helps pay hospital and doctor bills for older Americans. We also developed Medicaid, which finances health care for the poor, both young and old.

It is time to move further along the path of community to provide health coverage that is truly universal, and we cannot afford to abandon the idea simply because the Clinton administration's groundbreaking effort to enact fundamental health care reform failed. When a baby closes his eyes in a game of peekaboo, the other person doesn't really disappear. And the problems of our health care system haven't gone away just because the Republicans and Democrats are playing peekaboo with it.

Nearly 40 million Americans—over 80 percent of them in working households—remain uninsured, and millions more are at risk of losing insurance due to changes in the job market. On the other side, the rising costs threaten both government and private firms. And we all know those costs will continue to rise if for no other reason than the aging of our population.

Let's not kid ourselves: we should all understand by now that we're already paying for the uninsured. A homeless woman with diabetes but no health insurance probably gets no primary care; in that sense, we don't pay. But when she collapses on a city street, she's not left to die. She's taken to an emergency room and gets all the care she needs. Who pays? The rest of us. We pay because hospitals shift the costs of those who have no insurance onto the health bills of those who do. When we pay hospital bills or insurance premiums, we are absorbing the costs of the unreimbursed health care hospitals provide. Employers who provide health insurance to their employees wind up subsidizing employers who don't. That's unfair and untenable.

Even if we're not yet ready for comprehensive health reform, we can take steps to get our ailing health system into better shape.

If we aren't willing to ensure universal coverage for all Americans, we can at least provide it for our children. Currently, children in families receiving welfare are automatically eligible for Medicaid coverage. But the children of a day care worker or fast-food cook may get nothing. We rail against welfare dependency, but what would *you* do if the only way you could ensure that your little boy gets medical attention when he's sick is to stay on welfare? Would you, who love and cherish your own child more than anything in the world, be willing to try to lift yourself up by your bootstraps if it meant yanking your child away from health coverage? We need to find ways to extend health coverage to all our children, through a combination of public and private insurance.

We need to emphasize prevention, focusing on all the ways we can help people stay healthy, not merely how we can medicate them once they're ill. Promoting healthy habits like sensible eating and exercise would do more for the health of most Americans than any big-ticket, high-tech medical marvel. Prevention not only avoids suffering but also saves money. Programs that offer comprehensive prenatal care and supplemental nutrition to high-risk pregnant women pay for themselves many times over because they lead to healthier babies. Efforts like these should be expanded, as well as programs to vaccinate children against common infectious diseases, one of the most cost-effective and sensible health measures we can take, but one where we have a sorry record.

We need to reverse the priorities of our current health system. Instead of the small base of primary care and vast overcapacity for higher-cost specialized medicine that we now have, the system should provide a graduated continuum, starting with a broad base of primary, preventive, and public health services that lead as needed to a narrower band of high-level specialized care.

At every level of society, public and private, we must redouble efforts to prevent and treat substance abuse and addiction—"the most devastating health pandemic threatening our people," as former Health, Education, and Welfare Secretary Joseph Califano aptly describes it. Drugs, alcohol, and tobacco contribute to a medical house of horrors—heart disease, cancer, liver and kidney ailments; death and disfigurement from auto accidents, domestic violence, and street crime; AIDS and tuberculosis—costing society an estimated $200 billion. The 54 million Americans who smoke, the 20 million Americans who abuse drugs or alcohol, and the countless others affected by their destructive behavior weigh heavily on our health care system. It is imperative that we put more public funds into researching the causes of addictions and how to cure them, into massive efforts to prevent the young from seeking that first puff or that first high, and into treatment of the addicted of all ages.

Another important step: we can implement insurance reforms as we did in New York, where in 1992 we enacted the first community rating/open enrollment health insurance bill in the nation. Here's what that means, in plain English.

The business of insurance is one of spreading, or pooling, risks. In the case of health insurance, young, healthy people are low risks—they're unlikely to need costly medical care. People who are old or sick are high risks—they're likely to have large medical bills. Under community rating, low-, medium-, and high-risk people in the insurer's market are grouped together and pay the same rates, making it possible for all of them to get affordable coverage. This used to be the prevalent type of health insurance in America. But then commercial health insurers began "cherry picking." They began to differentiate between the low- and high-risk populations. They offered cut-rate premiums to young, healthy individuals and businesses with predominately young, healthy workers. And they began denying health insurance or imposing exorbitant rates on older or sick individuals or employers whose workers were older or had a history of health problems.

In the short term, that system—called experience rating—seemed like a good deal for some. But it had the impact of denying affordable coverage to the very people who need it most—as if insurers were only selling umbrellas on sunny days and refusing to sell them (or tripling the price) when it rained! And the nonprofit Blue Cross/Blue Shield insurers, who still used the old community rating system, got stuck with an increasing share of high-risk customers. No insurer can live with terms like that. You can't survive in the insurance business unless the expense of paying large claims to some policyholders is offset by premiums from other people with few claims.

And in the long run, it's not a good deal for anyone. One year, a healthy individual or a business with healthy employees might benefit from lower-cost insurance from an experience rater. But let that individual or some of the firm's employees develop serious illness, and the next year the same insurer might refuse to renew the policy, or jack up the rates. And since all of us are getting older, we are all heading down that road from low to high risk. What good is insurance that you can lose at the time you need it most? No better than the umbrella you bought in the sunshine but that dissolves into nothing the minute it starts to rain.

Another, related problem was the exclusion of preexisting conditions by commercial insurers. A woman recovering from breast cancer or a man with a record of heart trouble could be denied insurance outright, or the preexisting condition could be specifically excluded from their insurance policies. That's good for the insurer's bottom line, but not so good for anyone who gets seriously ill—the very people who most need health insurance.

To protect New Yorkers from these discriminatory practices, the state required that rates for all health policies sold to individuals and small businesses be determined using community rating. To ensure that sick people wouldn't be denied insurance coverage, New York's reforms included an open enrollment requirement for individual and small-business health insurance, meaning that no one can be excluded because of a preexisting condition. These changes do not in and of themselves bring about universal coverage, but they go a long way toward making insurance more widely available, and they are integral parts of the national health insurance provided by virtually every other industrialized nation in the world.

Finally, we should call on political leaders to present the facts to the American people, starting with the proposition that health reform must emphasize cost containment as well as expanded coverage. We need to cut unconscionable administrative costs and reduce redundant or excessive investment in costly medical technology. And we must retool our health system to make greater use of managed and coordinated care, which can provide proper health care at less cost.

The Social Challenge:
Stopping the Cycle of Catastrophe

As serious as our economic problems may be, the ugly tangle of our social vulnerabilities is perhaps even more daunting. Our celebrated strength and characteristic optimism are being sapped by a pervasive cultural corrosion, evidenced by everything from rising drug use to declining civility and moral standards. Republican responses to the situation seem to work on the theory that if only government is "tough" enough in these areas, the cavalry of personal responsibility will charge in and save the day; suddenly all the troubled people among us will shape themselves up and America will be America again.

Surely it's true that our social problems would largely disappear if we all conformed our conduct to the finest ideals of our civilization. On the other hand, while we need to take responsibility for ourselves, we are also responsible for each other. As James Madison once told us, "If men were angels, no government would be necessary." Because none of us is an angel, we need to use our collective strength, through government, not only to punish destructive behavior but to prevent it in the first place, and to help those who have fallen by the wayside put themselves back on track.

Welfare

In the national tug-of-war over family values and cultural corrosion, welfare is at the heart of the tussle, the big, tough knot that marks the middle of the rope and shows you which side is winning. Welfare, our shorthand for the initiative called Aid to Families with Dependent Children, is at its core an economic proposition, one of many programs we use to reach out to those members of our national community who have not, for whatever reason, been able to make it on their own. Welfare goes to families with children who do not have any other source of income; their modest checks from the government barely cover life's necessities. The conflict over welfare arises not because Americans have suddenly decided that it's a bad idea to help the less fortunate, but because the radical right has transformed the issue, with all its moral and practical complexity, into a blunt political wedge to divide the middle class against the poor.

The backers of the Contract start with the evidence that suggests that some rules we use to allocate welfare have mired some able-bodied adults in patterns of dependency that are costly for society and ultimately destructive for many of the recipients themselves. No argument there: in New York, we reached that conclusion as far back as 1986, with a groundbreaking study on the practical traps and perverse incentives built into the welfare system that led us to develop the first real alternative to welfare in the nation, New York's constructive and highly successful Child Assistance Program (CAP). Rather than providing similar constructive options, however, today's radical conservatives have chosen to turn some desperate young women and their children into scapegoats for all the rage and frustration of a nation racked by painful social and economic change.

I will make you one guarantee: we will never curse or castigate our way out of the welfare problem. Throwing people off the rolls might make welfare itself go away, but it won't make the problem go anywhere, because the real problem is poverty and the real solution is producing jobs and opportunity. Nevertheless, there are plenty of things wrong with the current welfare system. By all means, let's correct them, to make it fairer for everyone. Where should we start? Here are a few ideas and guiding principles:

- We should encourage states across the country to build on the most promising reforms already at work in places like New York, Maryland, and Colorado. The ingredients for success include passing tough laws to hold absent parents responsible for child support, and then making sure they actually pay by using sophisticated systems for matching computer records; making work a requirement for receiving benefits (though allowing commonsense exceptions for things like disability); providing skills training and child care so recipients can get and keep outside jobs; and relying on private placement firms to move participants into the workforce.

- We need to remove the perverse incentives. Perhaps the most important factor in the success of the CAP program in New York was that we eliminated the rule that said to welfare recipients, "For every dollar you earn in the marketplace, expect to lose a dollar in benefits." For people living on the edge of destitution, a rule like that meant that taking a job, which increased expenses like child care, transportation, and clothing, was just plain dumb. Changing the rule so they could keep more of what they earned gave them real incentive to try to lift themselves. We also recognized that just as some middle-income Americans may feel trapped in their jobs by the fear of losing health benefits, welfare recipients may be trapped in the program because it covers medical expenses for them and their children, while most entry-level jobs do not. Under CAP, we changed the rules to extend medical benefits for a period of time even after participants no longer qualified for formal welfare payments.

  Counterproductive incentives remain uncorrected across the country. We should move quickly to change that. We should ensure that welfare rules don't inadvertently weaken families by paying a single mother more if she lives alone with her children than if she lives with the children's father or stays with her own parents. To qualify for AFDC, unwed teenage mothers ought to be required to live with their parents and be prohibited from getting their own apartments, making humane exceptions, of course, for those who need to escape abusive homes. In addition, the benefits they receive should be in the form of food and clothing rather than cash.

- We should continue to give states the flexibility to experiment with sensible new reforms, rather than imposing rash changes from Washington. Despite all we have learned in the last few years about what combinations of incentives and disincentives can move welfare families into the mainstream and break the cycle of dependency, we do not yet know the perfect recipe. As we refine our approaches, we shouldn't rely solely on the self-serving claims of success by state officials competing for the title of "toughest on welfare." Instead, we should convene a single national blue-ribbon panel to evaluate the results of the various welfare experiments—to tell us which changes help and which hurt.
- We should establish federal safeguards to protect the poor from the possibility of cutting contests in which some states take unfair advantage of the new federal flexibility to balance their budgets on the backs of their poorest and least powerful citizens or to make their states inhospitable to the poor and drive them out.
- States should be wary of federal efforts to use devolution as an excuse for reducing the federal fiscal commitment to the programs that are essential to help welfare reform succeed. We should acknowledge that true welfare reform is not, in the short term, a money-saving strategy. It requires us to invest in things like job training, counseling, child care, and health benefits. Realistically, there's no other way to transform a young woman with little or no work history, few if any occupational skills, and several young children into a self-sufficient member of society.
- Finally, unless we use every means we have to fight fraud, abuse, and error, we will never rebuild confidence in the welfare program. In New York State, for example, we required recipients to be recertified at regular intervals. We also shared records with neighboring states to catch people who tried double dipping by applying for benefits in two or more locations.

Children Having Children

In the fight over welfare reform, the ugliest punches always seem to be thrown on the subject of unmarried teenage mothers. Republican answers run from harsh to very harsh, from no benefits for a second child born while the mother is on welfare, to no benefits for illegitimate children at all ever. Such responses punish children for the failures of their parents but fail to do anything about the peer pressure, hopelessness, and pinched horizons that can push teenage girls into sexual encounters and parental responsibilities they are nowhere near ready for. Once again, castigation will do no more than give us a catharsis.

We need to send our young people a message, certainly, about responsibility and self-restraint. But that same message must also say, "We love you. We care what happens to you. And we want to show you that you have better choices and other avenues to dignity." As long as their futures seem bleak, these girls will continue to try to fill the hole in their hearts with the love of a child, no matter how inconvenient we make it for them financially.

We need a new national effort to help them understand what a serious commitment parenthood is, help them get more out of school, and point them toward more promising futures. The best answer may be the oldest one: young people in trouble or headed that way need nothing so much as strong bonds to caring adults who have their own lives in order. For all too many girls at risk of becoming teen mothers, finding such a friend and guide on their own, in their own frail families and shattered neighborhoods, may be impossible. But it shouldn't be so hard for us to help them: one answer is to link them with mentors, adults from the larger community who volunteer to meet one-on-one with a child steadily through a year or more of adolescence. Does it work? In New York, our statewide, school-based mentoring program achieved impressive results in preventing school drop-outs and teen pregnancies. Continuing to build on the same school-based model, the not-for-profit Mentoring USA and other similar efforts are working well across the country, raising children's grades and their self-confidence. Now it's time to expand their scope to match our tremendous new needs, capitalizing on the organizing power of businesses and religious institutions as well as government and community-based not-for-profits.

We also need to look at both sides of the illegitimacy issue. There is a boy or a man behind each of these pregnancies, and we need to start sending the very clear message, through education and through the law, that a man who walks away from a child he has fathered is no kind of man at all. Tracking down unwed fathers and forcing them to bear their fair share of child-rearing costs is an important part of the answer.

Abortion and the Alternatives

Our goal should be not only to reverse the rise in illegitimacy and teen births, but to bring down the rate of teen pregnancy as well, because we will have done nothing good if our efforts indirectly cause a jump in the abortion rate.

. Probably none of us should expect in our lifetime a resolution to the argument over whether abortion should be permitted, restricted, or prohibited altogether. The issue has grown so polarized, in fact, that if we wish to move forward as a national community, we need to stop trying to talk or shriek or shoot our way to an answer on abortion and start focusing on the alternatives to it. No one on any side of the question can deny that the statistics on abortion are sobering. We should all be able to agree that 1.6 million abortions a year are too many, and that reducing unplanned or unwanted pregnancies—currently more than 3 million annually—would be a constructive step. What can we do to turn those numbers around?

To start with, all of us should take responsibility for teaching young men and women their responsibility in creating and caring for human life. Otherwise, we abdicate that role to the popular culture, which aims to entertain and amuse more than to teach and enlighten, and which is more apt to depict the joys of flirtation than the chores of changing diapers.

At the very least, adolescents and teenagers should hear from us that they are not abnormal because they choose to abstain from sexual relations until they are older, and perhaps until they are married. Planned Parenthood has found that a startling percentage of teen pregnancies result from girls being pressured into sex by males, often older than they. We need to teach young women ways to say no that won't make them feel cruel or impolite, and we must teach young men to respect that choice.

At the same time, we must recognize that not all young people will follow this preferred path, even with our best efforts. All young Americans should be made fully aware of the possible consequences of being sexually active. And it's more important today than ever that our public schools provide responsible sex education that recognizes and respects the variety of moral values and traditions in our society.

Contraception, for example, is an important point over which value systems diverge. The Catholic tradition teaches that the use of contraception is wrong, and those of us who are Catholic have a right to live by that belief; that kind of respect for differing viewpoints is one of the great beauties of this democracy. No one can be required to use contraception; no one can be required to have an abortion. However, for the sake of those people in our society who believe that contraception is an appropriate way to prevent unintended pregnancy, we should invest in developing better, easier, and safer methods of contraception.

And because the use of condoms in particular can prevent the spread of serious diseases, including AIDS, we cannot close our eyes to the consequences for our children's health. We may urge them to defer sexual relations, but if they choose to disregard our advice, use of a condom may save their lives, and we ought to make this message clear to them.

In order to make carrying their babies to term an appealing and realistic option for pregnant women who are considering abortion, adequate, affordable prenatal and neonatal medical care must be made more readily available and unnecessary barriers to adoption must be removed.

Finally, we should all be able to agree that a child's life beyond the womb deserves more consideration than it currently receives. Regardless of where a baby was born or under what circumstances, regardless of whether the parents are sixteen or thirty-six, married or not, when that new soul joins our American community, we have an obligation to see that the child has enough to eat, a roof overhead, the prospect of a decent education, and a chance to make a place in our economy.

Crime and Punishment

Fate has been generous with America in geography, resources, and material success. Yet a streak of brutality has marked our character from the beginning. Today, in the list of industrialized nations, we rank first in rates of murder, robbery, and rape. In the last twenty-five years, an unholy trio of factors has magnified America's long-standing propensity to violence, making us among the most violent people on earth. One is drugs: with just 5 percent of the world's population, we consume 50 percent of the world's cocaine, and humanity has never before had to defend itself against a drug as cheap and addictive as crack, or as likely to drive people to violence. The second factor: the increasing availability of high-powered weapons. The tough kids we used to call juvenile delinquents once fought with knuckles and knives; now they settle their quarrels fatally with AK-47s and "streetsweepers." The third, and least acknowledged piece of the puzzle, is the concentration of problems in overcrowded, effectively segregated ghettos where the sunlight of hope rarely shines, where stable families are the exception rather than the rule, where economic opportunity is at best a distant rumor, and where the most alluring male role models are the drug dealers and gang leaders.

These problems create burdens not only for those who fall prey to the lure of street violence and drugs, but for all too many of the rest of us as well—those who become victims of crime or of the fear of crime. The cost in human suffering is beyond calculation, but the cost in dollars is all too clear. The national hospital and medical bill for gunshot injuries alone is $4 billion every year. The overall cost of prisons and jails is $29 billion annually, and criminal justice is one of the fastest-growing parts of state budgets across the country. Indeed, the American Medical Association recently announced that violence is our "number one public health issue."

We need more effective law enforcement; on that, Democrats and Republicans are in full agreement. But we differ on how we hope to get it done. The Republicans propose to lead us toward greater harshness and brutality with the cure-all of tougher sentences and capital punishment; to lead us away from intelligent community control of lethal weapons and toward a "self-sufficient" vigilantism by repealing the Brady handgun law and the ban on assault weapons; and finally, to lead us away from the commonsense course of prevention, by scoffing at and actually scuttling programs specifically designed to shield vulnerable children and teenagers from the seductive temptations of crime.

In practical terms, this means that the radical right hopes to overturn key provisions of last year's popular crime bill, while Democrats want to take the ideas behind that new law and carry them even further. For example, it's a principle as old as criminal justice that what deters crime is not the harshness of a penalty but the sureness of its application, the certainty that violators will be both caught and punished. That's why President Clinton's crime bill was designed to put 100,000 more police on the streets. Without enough street officers, enough prosecutors, enough judges, enough cells, passing tough sentences is worse than meaningless. If there aren't enough police to catch the perpetrators, it magnifies the disrespect for law in general. If there aren't enough prison cells, it actually guarantees the kind of revolving-door justice for violent criminals that the Republicans were decrying even before they seized on Willie Horton.

An important step in rebuilding our national community will be restoring the safety of the streets we share, and there are a few steps we should focus on right away:

- We need to encourage sentencing reform nationwide to stop clogging state and federal prisons with nonviolent drug offenders. When we allocate scarce prison space to petty drug offenders, we leave the courts no room for jailing the violent

felons who pose the worst public threat. Currently, many juris-
dictions impose on persons convicted of selling small
amounts of drugs mandatory sentences that are longer than
those for people convicted of armed robbery—or even rape.
This has to change.

- We need to expand drug treatment programs both in and
  outside of prison, not dismantle them as Texas is now doing.
  The link between drugs and crime is as strong as the iron
  rings that hold together a ball and chain. In some state prison
  populations, 80 or 90 percent of inmates are estimated to have
  drug or alcohol problems, yet only a fraction of all prisoners—
  about 15 percent—are enrolled in drug treatment programs.
  Without stronger efforts to cure inmates of their addictions,
  our prisons become little more than a breeding ground for
  recidivists.

- We need to take a firm stand against Republican attempts to
  overturn the most intelligent gun control laws since we
  banned the Saturday Night Special: last year's Brady handgun
  law and the assault weapons ban.

- We must resist the hoarse chorus shouting for every possible
  expansion of capital punishment. I heard these shouts
  throughout my three terms as governor. Each year I was in
  office, I vetoed the bill that would have reimposed the death
  penalty. It was never a popular position, but it is one I have
  stated publicly and defended passionately for more than thirty
  years. I have watched as the numbers of those sentenced to
  death rises, and as Congress has tacked death penalties onto
  the U.S. criminal code every time it wants to look tough on
  crime. The new radical right enthusiasm for the death penalty
  exemplifies all that is wrong in today's political climate: harshness for its own sake, simplistic pseudosolutions, and a
  shameful pandering to popular misconceptions.

Frankly, despite what people tell the pollsters, I don't believe
it is the death penalty they want precisely; what they want is an
end to violent crime. The calls for capital punishment are really
a desperate demand that we do something more to stop the

nearly incredible brutality of recent years. It is a cry of anger born of frustration and fear, both feelings justified. But I'm convinced that responding to brutality with brutality will only make things worse.

Our passions are inflamed by each new terrible headline, by each appalling violation, by each savage murder of a law enforcement officer or a young mother or a hardworking grocery store owner gunned down for his petty cash. By the brazen, gun-toting drug dealers who terrorize the streets they think they own. By the madness of a Son of Sam or a Colin Ferguson. By the atrocities of terrorism increasingly close to home.

The people have a right to a civilized level of law and peace, and a right to be outraged when the world delivers horror and disorder instead. I understand the anger, the cries for retribution, even the desire for the ultimate revenge—"an eye for an eye," a death for a death.

I understand it, but I know something else. I know our society should strive for something better than what we are in our worst moments. I know that a civilized people must not descend willingly into darkness.

I have studied the death penalty since I was a law student. I have been in the death house and met prisoners sentenced to death. I have met with many who have lost relatives, friends, or co-workers to the malice of a murderer. I have reviewed all the arguments, both theoretical and practical. And I am surer now than I've ever been that the death penalty lowers us as a people; that while it does not deter violent crime, it is in itself an endorsement of brutality; that it is applied so erratically as to be inherently unfair; that it will surely kill innocent people; and that it is more expensive but no more effective than life in prison without parole.

As a deterrent, the death penalty is surprisingly ineffective. No persuasive evidence exists that official state killing will make our citizens, or even our police officers, safer. There is, in fact, evidence to the contrary. For the decade before 1977, we had the death penalty in New York State. In that period, eighty police officers were slain. In the decade after, with no death penalty, the number dropped to fifty-four. Most recently, in the first six months of 1995, the murder rate in New York City declined by nearly one-third, without the death penalty.

The argument for deterrence is further weakened by the realization of how rarely and unpredictably capital penalties are applied. When legal sanctions are effective, it is not because they are harsh as much as that they are certain. And the death penalty has always been terribly unsure. During the past decade, execution occurred in only about five-hundredths of one percent of all the homicides committed in this country.

There is actually reason to believe that some madmen, like serial killer Ted Bundy, may even be tempted to murder because of a perverse desire for their own death. For many, the prospect of life in prison without parole is a far more frightening and horrible prospect than death itself. Don't believe me? Take it from Thomas Grasso, a man convicted for murder in two states, Oklahoma and New York. As I interpreted the law, he was required to serve his lifetime sentence in New York, but my successor as governor chose to permit Grasso's extradition to Oklahoma, a state with the death penalty. On the morning of his execution, Grasso said, "Let there be no mistake, Mario Cuomo is right: life without parole is much worse than the death penalty."

Death penalty proponents ignore another horrifying fact. Our criminal justice system is not perfect. It makes mistakes. The causes are many: the overly ambitious prosecutor, the sloppy detective, the incompetent defense counsel, the witness who is biased or simply mistaken. Each year some men and women are imprisoned for crimes they didn't commit. When the error or injustice is discovered, they are set free. But when a person is wrongly executed, there is no way the state can give back the life. Since the turn of the century, at least twenty-three people are believed to have been wrongly executed in the United States. These were innocent people, murdered by the government under color of law.

Conviction of criminal defendants is based on proof beyond a reasonable doubt—not proof to an absolute certainty. Yet proponents of the death penalty are seeking to broaden dramatically the cases in which we can impose the most absolute, irreversible penalty mankind can inflict. We should reject their bid for a new American brutality and demand something wiser: a real, tough effective punishment for deliberate murder. One that juries will not be reluctant to impose. One that by some estimates costs only a third of the total price of a capital prosecution. One that does not require us to be infallible in order to avoid taking innocent life. One that does not require us to stoop to the level of the killer. That penalty is true life imprisonment, with no possibility of parole. If you commit a murder at twenty and live to be eighty, you'll spend six decades behind bars. You'll never come out alive. Now that's a tough penalty. As we've heard from many inmates, the thought of having to live a whole lifetime behind bars, only to die in your cell, is even worse than death.

When we hear the calls for a return to capital punishment, the most primitive form of justice, those of us who object have an obligation to resist, especially when resistance is unpopular, as it is today. At times like this, we need to remind ourselves that the real story of human progress has always been a tale of unexpected triumphs and sudden reversals. It has always proceeded in fits and starts. But it has, on balance, been a story of inexorable gains, inching forward and upward toward the light. Reembracing the death penalty, a sanction illegal in every other industrialized country and now even in South Africa, is a step backward for our national community, and we must do everything we can to see that this backward step does not begin a downward trend.

Prevention

Fighting criminals in the street with the relentless enforcement of firm laws and with swift, sure punishment is inarguably necessary and appropriate. But just as important—and a lot less expensive in all ways—would be keeping people from being lured into lives of crime. We can't solve the problem with police and prisons. Effective law enforcement is necessary but not sufficient. We need to be tough on crime, certainly, but we need to be equally tough on the *causes* of crime. This is where Republican strategies fall woefully, tragically short.

Like governors across the country in the 1980s, I was forced
to respond to rising crime and a swelling prison population with
more police and prisons than ever before. But that was not, and
will not, be enough to stop crime in New York or anywhere else.
We should always apply the law firmly, but we must also give
people avenues to dignity instead of streets to despair. We need
to offer prevention as well as punishment, carrots as well as
sticks. Republicans are already persuaded of the power of carrots in other areas; if they would like us to believe that tax cuts
will encourage business to grow, shouldn't we also believe that
giving vulnerable children safe, interesting, constructive alternatives to gangs and drugs might encourage them to grow?

It just makes no sense, intellectually, philosophically, or economically, to deal with crime only by focusing on detention,
apprehension, and punishment. Common sense tells us that prevention is always a good idea, and experience tells us that it's
usually cheaper in the long run.

Imagine a village where more and more of the young people
were being driven crazy by drinking from a poisoned lake in the
hills. They storm the village night after night, creating mayhem.
More and more of them are locked up. More and more executed.
The villagers have to pay for more and more police and jail cells.
Wouldn't someone say "Let's dry up the lake; let's find a new
source of clean water"?

Tragedies like drug addiction, violence, children having children, broken families, and rampant crime are not visited upon
us like earthquakes and floods, but are, uniformly, avoidable
disasters. What's more, there are a lot of good things we should
be doing to avoid them. We need to provide adequate drug
treatment, counseling, and mentoring services for troubled teens,
and recast our schools as real community centers, refuges from
the pressures of the outside world. We need to help parents
take more responsibility for their own children by making safe,
affordable day care and parenting education widely available,
and by working with employers to develop things like flextime
arrangements. We need to support, not ridicule, programs that
keep kids off the streets and out of trouble, teach sportsmanship,
and enable them to channel their aggressive energies into the

playful combat of sports rather than the mortal combat of the streets.

These efforts at prevention will never be enough, however, unless we tackle the vexing questions of poverty, income inequality, unemployment, and racial discrimination—toxins that poison a community and make young people more prone to crime. When the social norms offer nothing positive to a young man, should it surprise us if his conduct slides toward the antisocial? Reducing poverty and unemployment will ultimately do more to reduce crime and rebuild our communities than all the tough sentencing laws we could ever devise.

Beyond addressing specific problems like drugs and teen pregnancy, effective prevention demands a broader commitment to strengthening our families and communities. Today, when the majority of children live either with only one parent or in a family where both parents work outside the home, we need to help people balance the demands of work and parenting. And our commitment to education, from preschool on, must be part of our long-term crime-fighting equation. A child excited about learning is a child who will find school more appealing than the street corner.

Finally, we need to face the delicate challenge of relieving the self-perpetuating problem of ghetto density. When we jam together and isolate the most troubled people in our society, we often end up with neighborhoods bereft of positive role models, where overcrowding makes the basic degradations of poverty intolerable to the point of violence. As sociologist D. Stanley Eitzen has noted: "Where [adverse conditions] converge, they interact to increase crime rates. Thus, there is a relatively high probability of criminal behavior—violent criminal behavior— among young, black, impoverished males in inner cities where poverty, unemployment, and racial segregation are concentrated."

We need to look at a range of possible solutions, things like rezoning sites once they become vacant or refraining from building more low-income housing where too much already exists. To help low-income families leave the ghettos behind, we need to provide portable vouchers, promote scatter-site housing, and offer "equity assurance" to make middle-class neighborhoods more receptive to mixed-income development by guaranteeing their property values.

These are all good ideas, and they only begin to suggest the universe of things we can do to defeat crime and despair before they snuff out the soul of another child. To everything there is a season, however. Just because we want to do everything in our power to inspire and encourage young people to do right does not mean we should be soft on those who nevertheless do wrong. I was reminded of this when I was no more than nineteen or twenty, working at a summer camp in upstate New York.

The camp was for boys from Brooklyn and Queens and Manhattan who were already in trouble, kids from about nine or ten to about sixteen. I had already finished one year of college and had spent a summer on the farm team for the Pittsburgh Pirates, meaning that by the standards of the campers I was a big success. My reward? The tent with the really hard cases, the oldest kids, the toughest kids, the ones you weren't sure you wanted to turn your back on. The worst of them all was Johnny, one of the older kids—not just bad, but *mean* bad.

We had a young seminarian working with us—Paul Coletti. He had come over from Italy to be a priest and decided to work at the camp one summer for some practical experience. Paul Coletti couldn't swim, which was okay, except that he told the boys about it. One day Paul was down by the pool with the rest of us, and Johnny came up behind him and deliberately pushed him into the deep end. Paul panicked. I couldn't swim all that well, either, but I jumped in and managed to get the poor guy out, half-drowned.

I was not, at that age, inclined to the kind of pacifism and charity that Paul had committed himself to, and Johnny was so arrogant when I talked to him afterward that I wanted to belt him. Apparently I didn't disguise that fact very well. My reward for that from Father Logatto, the great old priest who ran the camp, was a detailed sermon that evening on the virtue of patience. I said, "Father, I'm just not that good."

The next day, however, the story was different. I happened to see Father Logatto and Johnny encounter each other on a path.

They talked for a while. Then Father reached out to Johnny and put his hand on his shoulder. Johnny slapped it away. What did Father Logatto do? He kicked Johnny in the behind so hard that Johnny wound up in the bushes. After it was all over, I went up to the old priest with a question. "Father, what happened to the virtue of patience?" "Mario," he said, "there is a time for patience . . . and there is a time for instruction."

I regretted getting angry, and so did Father Logatto. But it's clear that if we hope to rebuild the strength of our people and the foundation of our national community, we will need big applications of both patience and firmness.

A Crusade for Values

There is among the American people a growing unease with the harshness, the coarseness, the violence, depravity, and obsessive sexual emphasis of American life. What should we do about it? Is there any way we can force ourselves, or persuade ourselves, to behave better as a people—to end the violence, reject the brutality, accept responsibility, learn to love?

If we are failing to handle the responsibility for civility ourselves, can government do it *for* us? Of course not. But government can certainly help. Ultimately, like a driver at the wheel, each of us determines whether our car is driven safely. But government posts speed limits, passes laws against recklessness, insists that we have our brakes inspected. And government either enforces the rules it imposes, reinforcing our better instincts, or it grows lax, inviting irresponsible behavior. Some of society's rules clearly need to be enforced more effectively—like the laws that reinforce the responsibility to work for your own bread and provide for your own children. Laws that require that everyone who *can* work must work as a condition for receiving welfare assistance. Laws that help make sure absent parents pay child support.

Government can also take steps that are positive affirmations of what we do believe in. When we say education is important, government can prove we really mean it, by committing adequate funds. Wouldn't it be nice if schools had all the computers and science equipment and art supplies they needed, the way the military has billions for state-of-the-art weapons of destruction—billions more even than they ask for? We don't require the Pentagon to hold bake sales to fund the armed forces; why should our schools have to beg for a few extra dollars for our children's education? Government can also support the arts and humanities and public radio and television, which give every part of the American community access to experiences that enrich and enlighten us, enhance our appreciation for all that is good and beautiful, and underscore values that help elevate our level of civility.

At the very least, we should make sure that our laws do not tear at the fabric of the values we cherish, as has happened with welfare regulations that inadvertently discourage parents from living together or give a teenage girl with a child an incentive to move out of her parents' home. Properly done, reform of our national welfare laws can encourage, perhaps even inspire, people to do good things for themselves—finish school, keep their families together, and work their way to independence.

But there is a limit to what we can compel by law. As Lincoln reminded us in his formulation of government, some things we can do only—or do better—for ourselves. There are some things government cannot make us do, even with the fiercest laws and the most vigorous enforcement. Tough laws can slow the supply of drugs, but unless there is an end to the demand for drugs— the original decision to invite the addiction in—there cannot be enough law to save us. We can't expect government alone to win the war on illegal drugs, as long as Americans in large numbers keep choosing to buy and use them.

So, too, with offensive sex and violence on television and in the movies and popular music. Should government have a role in cleaning up the garbage that pours out of the popular culture and into our living rooms and our children's hearts? We see our media emphasizing fast action, cheap thrills, and instant gratification, we see ugliness and vulgarity blatantly displayed, magnified, and glorified in the mass media, and we hope wistfully that by erasing distasteful images from the movie or television screen or the compact disc we might be able to eradicate them from our culture. Under the circumstances, why shouldn't the government intervene? Is the problem not serious enough?

There is no question that the media's unbridled re-creation of all this madness induces a certain amount of irrationality, especially among our children and vulnerable adults. In our mass culture, television and movies and popular music feed the cultural reservoir we all drink from and are influenced by. So the cries for government intervention are not surprising, if for no other reason than it would give us a sense of doing something about a problem that seems hopelessly out of control.

Fortunately, new technologies like the V-chip, which enables parents to block out certain programs or categories of programs to protect their children, may offer us indirect and acceptable avenues for constructive government action. Without endangering the Constitution, we can certainly insist that broadcasters create and apply a movie-style rating system and that manufacturers build V-chips into all future television sets.

But we must resist absolutely the temptation for any brand of more direct government intervention. It would mean giving grandstanding politicians or faceless bureaucrats the power to decide what should be written or produced or seen or heard. In addition to raising grave First Amendment concerns, it would be hopelessly impractical. Who would be wise enough to decide which violence was okay and which was morally destructive? What standards would they use to censor what we see and hear? Would news coverage of war atrocities and vicious real-life crimes be appropriate, but not fictionalized accounts of murder and mayhem? Or would it be the other way around? Would violence inflicted by heroes be treated the same as the violence of villains? Should the main test be the context of the violence or how graphic or realistic it is? What about slapstick cartoon violence, the kind Bugs Bunny and Elmer Fudd inflict upon each other? Too violent? How about opera or professional wrestling? Or Arnold Schwarzenegger or William Shakespeare?

That leads us to another option. Shouldn't we simply call upon the media themselves to practice self-restraint? Shouldn't we just urge broadcasting and movie and music executives to exercise their First Amendment freedoms responsibly and use their influence to inspire us instead of debase us? Shouldn't we remind them that the right to free speech does not imply an obligation to be as offensive as possible, and that when they push the limits of public tolerance, they should not be surprised if they provoke repressive responses?

Yes, we should, and I do—right here. But no matter how eloquent our arguments, self-policing by business will have only limited effect. Like all business, media companies function in a profit-driven free enterprise system. Their main obligation, their fiduciary duty, is to produce profits for their shareholders. Few of them recognize any moral obligation beyond that—even if some politicians insist they should.

The ultimate truth, I think, should make us a lot more uncomfortable. If we agree that government censorship is impermissible and self-policing relatively ineffective, we must also agree that any effort to clean up the airwaves and other media will have to start much closer to home, with *us*. The executives of movies and TV and music aren't jamming sex and violence and profanity down our throats. The American people are choosing it from an ever-expanding menu. The viewers, not the producers, boost the ratings of the titillating kiss-and-tell TV talk shows in which people announce to an audience of two million strangers sins that people of my generation would have been ashamed to whisper in the privacy of a confessional. The music-buying public, including millions of suburban kids from what we would be quick to call "good" homes, eagerly buy gangsta rap CDs with vulgar and vitriolic lyrics. We the people—we ordinary Americans—buy the tickets for the blockbuster films in which murder, mayhem, car crashes, and explosions occur at the same rapid pace that once characterized the witty banter between Nick and Nora or Tracy and Hepburn. We're the ones with the lust for sex and blood, scandal and perversion. We are the ones caught in this uncomfortable contradiction: the desire for what disgusts us, the disgust for what we desire.

Any effort to clean up the airwaves, the movies, or the music we consume will have to start with us—changing what we watch, what we buy, what we ask for. In the end, we must choose to make better choices.

A television network or a Hollywood studio will offer us virtually whatever material vast numbers of people will watch. They're businesses designed to make a profit; we can no more expect them to substitute thoughtful documentaries for bloody cops-and-robbers shows than imagine that McDonald's will overlook our appetite for french fries and high-mindedly insist that we accept side orders of spinach instead.

But let's stay with that analogy for a moment. In the last few years, salads have suddenly appeared on the menus of McDonald's and the other burger-and-fries establishments. Why? Because consumers asked for healthier alternatives, and customers generally get what they ask for. Perhaps the most efficient way to improve the quality of radio and television, as well as movies and popular music, would be the purest kind of commercial persuasion, a real self-help campaign by consumers. A decision to tune out the garbage, perhaps even to boycott the sponsors. A concerted national effort to tell the media and one another that we want something better than the worst our culture has to offer.

If it's clear that we cannot legislate our way out of the moral miasma of the media, it should be equally clear that the trail upward to a stronger, sweeter culture will not be carved with the tools of government action. If we choose to solve this problem together, there are surely ways we can call on government to help us get the job done. But for the most part it is a transformation we must achieve ourselves.

We need to think of ourselves as a family. We need to give our children an example so big and sweet and joyful that they can be brave in the face of degradation and emptiness. We need to envelop them in the warmth of our national ideals, as my parents enveloped me in their love, taught me fairness and a sense of responsibility, and offered their own eloquent examples of hard work, humility, self-sacrifice, and persistence.

What if it were your child, or children in your neighborhood, whom you were trying to save from drug dealers, weapon-wielding marauders, reckless sex, and all kinds of disorientation? What would you do? Would you leave a note on the refrigerator once every couple of weeks? Talk to your son once a year, "man-to-man"? Hope that your daughter learned enough about AIDS from the pamphlet you left on the coffee table?

Or would you do everything, all at once, all the time? Everything you could to protect and instruct and inspire them to make the right judgments in a world that offers all too many bad choices.

To leave our children a world worth inheriting, what we need is nothing less than an all-out, pervasive, constant effort by every part of the community we can enlist to demonstrate, by the example of conduct, the things we value, and why. The inspiration needs to spring from everywhere—the family, the school, the neighborhood, and all the houses of worship; businesses and political leaders; and the great power of our entertainment industry. And some of the steps are so simple they could happen tomorrow, if only we believed in our own powers. How about these ideas, just for starters:

We should make sure all parents have access to the materials they need at home to teach values like compassion and compromise, and encourage communities to set up neighborhood patrols composed of ordinary citizen-volunteers. We should urge our business leaders to consider giving special bonuses to any employee who serves as a mentor to a child and call on leaders of the entertainment industry to see that all major performing arts awards include a community service category, as the Emmy Awards do now.

At our churches, temples, mosques, and meeting halls, we should speak out against drugs every time services are held, and we should encourage the same institutions to consider "adopting" a local public school, to provide tutors, mentors, or other assistance, not only to extend practical help, but also to reinforce a powerful web of community feeling.

The overwhelming majority of Americans want our schools to instruct children in values like honesty, democracy, tolerance, patriotism, and moral courage. Why not insist that every school day begin with some teaching of basic values, including the willingness to restrain appetites, to discipline desires, to accept responsibility?

Why do many Catholic academies succeed in troubled neighborhoods where public schools often fail? As much as I love my faith, I don't think it's necessary to attribute the success to a superiority of dogma. A more practical reason will do, as one recent study concluded. At least part of the secret is that the students, the parents, and the staff share a community of values, "a broad set of beliefs about what students should learn, how to conduct themselves, and what kind of people they should become."

We should encourage every public school to develop such a community of values, building on the basic principles of our civil society and expressed through a new companion for the national Pledge of Allegiance—a special "Pledge of Purpose" devised by the members of each school community, to outline their common values, goals, and responsibilities.

Let's face it, though. Especially with respect to already disadvantaged children, the parents, the private sector, the schools, and the houses of worship may find it difficult to supply all the education that's needed.

By far the strongest educational force in our society is the electronic media. Isn't that why they have become the objects of our condemnation, because we suspect they are, to a dangerous extent, teaching our children bad things? As political scientist Curtis Gans once noted, "[T]elevision . . . is to conventional means of communication what nuclear weaponry is to conventional weaponry." If we really want to reach the young, the perplexed, the vulnerable, we can't stop until we have enlisted the most powerful teacher at our disposal.

We should start by influencing the programming, for certain—talking to executives and writers, trying to get each person to take responsibility for the day-to-day decisions that shape what we see and hear. We should urge public companies to spend part of their commercial advertising dollars to run prime-time advertisements against drugs and violence and antisocial behavior. And if we can't persuade the entertainment industry to cooperate with us voluntarily, why can't groups of shareholders raise the subject of violence and destructive programming at the annual corporate meeting, every year, until we see a change?

And we can also do something more direct. We may not like

to confess it, but our nation is second to none at the television commercial—and as a medium it may be useful for something other than selling us four-wheel-drive vehicles and cold-filtered beer. As one commentator explained, "The television commercial is the most efficient, power-packed capsule of education that appears anywhere on TV." We have a cadre of highly creative people who specialize in producing irresistible arguments guaranteed to influence attitudes and behavior in a minute or less. Can't we get these folks playing for our team?

We have already begun to tap this resource—through admirable efforts like the Partnership for a Drug-Free America and MTV's Enough-Is-Enough campaign against violence. But we need a response that's more comprehensive; we need to make the message inescapable. We can't be satisfied with a handful of public service announcements that run every once in a while, or at two in the morning. Without a major commitment, we actually trivialize the message.

But perhaps you think that the idea itself is silly, that it can't work, that TV can't influence behavior. Really? Tell that to the soap manufacturers and auto executives who spend hundreds of millions of dollars buying television time to shape what we desire and what we buy. Tell it to the political candidates, who regularly attribute lost races to the fact that their opponent had "more money for TV." Or tell it to the State of California, which ran a massive campaign of saturation TV advertising that made measurable progress against teenage smoking.

I'm convinced that we can make television work for us. It's time that we develop a program, backed by federal and state money, to buy time on the major broadcast and cable networks, particularly during the hours children will be watching, to teach values like honesty, loyalty, tolerance, responsibility. To offer instruction against violence and racism and drugs. To run the funniest, most entrancing, most beautiful spots you've ever seen —all of them advertising the wonder of life, the beauty of our democracy, the power of hard work and aspiration.

If we do it right, our children might finally believe that we mean what we say about family values, because we will have demonstrated conclusively that we value the family of America.

Dealing with the Deficit

Our nation faces a difficult dilemma. As this chapter has described, the federal government needs to make investments to help boost the economy and repair our torn social fabric. But at the same moment, we also need to reduce the budget deficit to get our fiscal house in order. Squeezed by this conflict of priorities, our elected officials have for too long tried to wriggle out of it, as though federal budget policy were a Houdini escape trick, or resorted to blue smoke and mirrors, dazzling us like a Siegfried and Roy illusion. The result of all of this political manipulation, however, is anything but an illusion: a huge debt of $5 trillion and annual deficits 400 percent higher than they were in the Carter years.

Most of the heavy damage was done during the Reagan years. After enacting tax cuts, Republicans insisted on raising defense spending to unprecedented levels, while Democrats, after a couple of years of giving in, resisted Republicans' further efforts to slash domestic spending. The result: tax-and-spend was replaced by borrow-and-spend.

Today, however, the Republicans and the Democrats both say we need to cut the deficit. In his first year President Clinton was able to make a dent in the problem with the help of a Democratic Congress. Now the Republican Congress has proposed to balance the budget within an arbitrarily fixed period —seven years—while at the same time enacting massive tax cuts. The result would be draconian slashes in important programs like Medicare. The President says, let's go slower—make it ten years—and limit the tax breaks so that we can avoid the most severe Medicare cuts and maybe even have enough to invest where we need to in education, health care, and help for children.

I believe the President has the better side of the case, but he does not go far enough. There is no wisdom in going from inexcusable laxity to arbitrary rigidity. Although we need to lower the deficit, we do not need to shrink it to zero within any specific fixed period. During the prosperous, productive 1950s and 1960s we typically ran a deficit, though a small one, hovering around one percent of the GDP.

Reducing the deficit is never easy. There are three ways to do it—cut spending, raise taxes, or luck out and benefit from the growth in the economy. Moderate growth is continuing and that's good, but too uncertain to constitute a complete strategy. Raising taxes is out of the question politically—at least for the moment. The real option is to cut spending, and that's always difficult. Although the public supports deficit reduction in the abstract, the only spending they want to see cut is spending for someone else's program; none of us should be surprised by human nature. The real problem, however, is that this unbecoming tendency has been so magnified by the political process that it's obstructing any real progress toward spending less. Here's how it works:

Imagine a federal program that exists solely to provide subsidies to a thousand turnip growers, most of whom are concentrated in two or three states. The program costs $5 million a year. Economists and nonpartisan analysts conclude the subsidies serve no valid public interest. The average voter favors deficit reduction and wouldn't object to curbing turnip subsidies but doesn't spend so much as a nanosecond thinking about the subject, much less taking the time to write or call Congress to demand an end to all future turnip supports. On the other hand, every turnip grower and turnip processor leaps into action; the Washington lobbyists for the American Turnip League work day and night; the turnip industry's political action committee (PAC) calls on those who have benefited from its campaign contributions; the representatives from key turnip districts and senators from key turnip states flex whatever political muscle they have to save the program. There is no counterweight; no lobbyist whose full-time job is to defeat turnip subsidies. Result: the turnip subsidy program survives. Multiply this kind of situation a thousand times over, and you see how hard it is to reduce federal spending or to control the federal budget.

Precisely because it is so difficult to reduce the deficit, we need to understand why we so urgently have to do it.

The Republican ideology views deficit reduction almost with glee. Instinctively favoring individualism over community, they view much of what our government does to help people as intrinsically wasteful, inherently suspect, and inevitably detrimental. To them, cutting domestic programs is like shedding a bad habit.

I see the matter differently. I believe that even though many of the programs destined for cutbacks or elimination serve a beneficial purpose, we need to reduce the deficit because the greater good of the community, including that of future generations, requires us to impose tighter fiscal discipline right away and for a long time to come. Excessive deficits drain the nation of the capital we need to save and invest in order to promote long-term economic growth and protect our standard of living.

Economists usually try to explain how this works in megadollars, what they call macroeconomic terms. They talk about the overall U.S. savings rate, the percentage of our $7 trillion economy that goes to investment, and so forth. For many of us, this is about as helpful as trying to glean tomorrow's weather forecast from a climatology lecture. Let's bring it to a more basic level.

Think of a street peddler who starts out with nothing but $50 and a pushcart. Five mornings a week he goes to the wholesale fruit market and purchases $50 worth of produce, which he sells at a modest profit, every nickel of which goes to cover his room and board. With no savings, he starts out at square one economically each week, with the same pushcart, and the same $50 to buy his modest inventory of fruit. With no savings and thus no capital, he has no way to expand his business or raise his standard of living.

Then, determined to make a change, the peddler begins to scrimp and sacrifice and cut his expenses to the bone, so that he's able to put aside some money each week—not much, but at the end of one year he has $2,000 in the bank. That's his capital, and he plows it back into his business. He uses part of the money to buy a larger pushcart and the rest to stock the cart with more merchandise. Now he's selling more and earning more while still keeping his living expenses to a minimum. That means he can put aside more money, and within a year he's saved $5,000. The next year, he can afford to lease a hot dog stand and hire an employee to run it. Now he's bringing in more money than ever. But it was only because he accumulated savings in the first place that he was able to move ahead economically.

On a national level, the situation is similar, with one big difference. We don't expect each business to rely only on its own savings to finance its growth. Companies borrow from banks, or sell stock to investors. But where do the banks get their money? From money their depositors have saved. Where do investors get the money to buy stocks? From their savings. If no one saved, there would be no money on deposit for banks to lend, no money in investors' hands to buy stock, and no way for businesses to obtain the capital they need. When our overall rate of savings is too low, the pool of available capital is too shallow.

So how does this relate to the budget deficit? When the government runs large deficits, it reduces the nation's net savings and puts itself in competition for available capital. As a result, capital becomes more scarce or, as interest rates rise, more expensive, and companies can't obtain the capital they need to grow and generate jobs.

Equally important is the composition of government outlays. Prudent public investments can raise productivity and generate economic growth much the way private sector investments do. Unfortunately, our government is devoting far too little of its budget to investment. Only 2.6 percent of last year's federal outlays were for education and training, down from 5.0 percent in 1975. Only 1.9 percent of the federal budget went to nondefense research and development, down from 2.7 percent in 1975. Only 3.6 percent went for infrastructure, down from 4.8 percent twenty years ago. So we must reorder our spending priorities as we reduce overall spending growth.

Another reason we must reduce the deficit is to prevent our growing debt from swamping our children and grandchildren and lowering their standard of living. The more debt we leave to them, the greater the portion of their income that will be siphoned off each year to service that debt—in other words, to pay for things that *we* consumed. And that will leave them with less to spend and even less to invest.

How do we control the deficit?

First, we can acknowledge that we do not have to do it as rapidly as has been proposed, nor to set our sights on zero. Meeting those goals would inflict unacceptable pain in the short run—possibly even triggering a recession—and would shortchange the public investments that benefit us in the long run. Besides, recent history proves that unrealistic budget goals simply do not work. In 1985, we attempted to place government spending in a legislative straitjacket with the Gramm-Rudman-Hollings bill, which promised to eliminate the deficit over a five-year period, but it soon became apparent that government simply could not function within those rigid constraints. By 1987, compliance with the Gramm-Rudman-Hollings targets was virtually impossible. So what did we do? We amended the legislation to move the balanced budget goalpost to 1993. That didn't work out either. The actual deficit for 1993 was $255 billion! Rather than repeat this sort of charade or compound it by raising it to the level of an amendment to the Constitution, we should aim to reduce the deficit as fast as reasonably possible, while at the same time doing all the other things we have to do, like controlling the growth in taxes and making vital investments in infrastructure, education, defense, health care, and other necessities.

Second, we must avoid missteps that make the budget problem even worse than it already is.

We should realize that as politically desirable as they may be, this is no time for tax cuts. They would have either of two consequences, both harmful. Either the deficit will swell, or the revenue losses will have to be offset with spending reductions so severe that they will damage the well-being of our people. Neither the Republicans' audaciously irresponsible tax cuts, which would cost $245 billion over seven years, nor the Clinton administration's more modest but still unaffordable $105 billion cuts deserve to be adopted. Cutting taxes at the same time you're trying to reduce the deficit makes as much sense as starting a trip to the east by marching in the direction of the setting sun.

Similarly, we should reject Republican plans to increase military spending, which are more than is warranted in the post–Cold War era, and even more than the Pentagon experts insist they need. In this year's budget alone, Republican leaders sought to add $7 billion to the Pentagon's budget to sprinkle tasty projects throughout politically connected districts. While one can sympathize with defense industry employees and communities affected by base closings, it's time to reorient the public investments in swords we no longer need and shift them into profitable plowshares.

Third, budget cutting requires shared sacrifice. No one is eager to sacrifice and people will certainly refuse to if they think that others are unfairly escaping the obligation. Budgetary sacred cows should all be de-sanctified. From congressional pensions to farm subsidies, all areas of the budget must be carefully scrutinized and reformed. One area where we can achieve substantial savings, for example, is slashing corporate welfare, the spending subsidies and tax breaks granted to particular companies or industries more on the basis of political clout than on rational economics.

Fourth, we can continue efforts already under way to reinvent government—finding ways for government to accomplish its mission with greater efficiency and at less cost.

Last but most important, we must tackle the politically thorny question of the non-means-tested entitlements like Medicare (which the Republicans have already put on the table) and Social Security (which they have not). Simply put, our present course is unsustainable. As last year's Kerrey-Danforth Commission reported, under present policy, by the year 2012—roughly a decade and a half from today—outlays for entitlements plus interest on the national debt will consume every last tax dollar the federal government collects. There will literally be nothing left over for national defense, education, highways, disease control, economic development, or anything else.

Demanding our particular attention is Medicare. The Medicare

trust fund that finances health care for the elderly requires immediate reform, not only to help cut the deficit but also to save
the program itself. Unless we begin now to control Medicare
spending, the trust fund will be broke by 2002. If we sit on our
hands and wait for the crisis, the consequences will be so ugly
that we won't need term limits to get rid of a whole Congress
worth of incompetent politicians; the voters will do it themselves.

Although Social Security's peril is not as immediate, its problems, and their ramifications for the overall federal budget, are
equally daunting. We need to make big changes if we want to
preserve basic Social Security benefits in the face of the dramatic
demographic pressure caused by the aging of the Baby Boomers
and longer life expectancies. By 2030, there will be twice as
many Americans over the age of seventy as there are today, and
the Social Security trust fund will be utterly depleted. Well before
then, sometime during the second decade of the next century,
paying benefits to our retirees will require drawing down the
surplus that we have been steadily building in the trust fund. At
that time, the trust fund will no longer be able to purchase
Treasury bonds as it does now, which will force the federal
government to borrow additional funds from the public, com-
pounding our deficit problem.

What can be done to restrain the growth in entitlements?
There is no shortage of options. Lists have rained down from
congressional committees, blue-ribbon panels, think tanks, and
policy analysts from every segment of the political spectrum. For
Social Security, options include limiting annual cost of living
adjustments (COLAs), gradually increasing the age of eligibility
for full retirement benefits, and modifying the way benefits are
pegged to past wages. For Medicare, we have choices like making greater use of cost-effective managed care, modifying payments to health providers, and increasing the Part B premiums
paid by beneficiaries. All of these options, and many others,
need to be considered, but the ultimate solutions should be
designed so that the neediest are protected. For example, we
could reduce Social Security COLAs and increase Medicare premiums only for comparatively affluent retirees.

The absolute necessity for entitlement reforms and the options to accomplish them are well known by Washington's policy makers, politically connected insiders, and elected officials. At dinner parties, cocktail receptions, and symposiums, they all say, "We have to do something, but the people won't let us. And the President and Congress have no choice but to do what the people want, even if the people are misinformed."

The truth is, politicians will refuse to touch entitlements until we as citizens tell the pollsters that we want our representatives to bite the bullet. Realistically, we can't call on Congress or the President to act while at the same time we tell them—through the polls—that we'll boot them out of office at the next opportunity if they do. Search high and low, but you'll find few saints or martyrs in the chambers of Congress. Most of them put prudence before valor. Many of them simply reason: "You can't be a leader without any followers. And you can't be an elected leader if you're voted out of office."

More than anything, we need to decide what we want our elected officials to do. Washington can't both close the budget gap and keep the entitlement spigot flowing freely. We, the people, have to speak up—especially the young people whose economic security is most at risk. We ought to tell the pollsters: we want Washington to do the right thing and curb entitlement spending in a meaningful and fair way.

But what if the people don't raise their voices for prudence and action? The system will remain paralyzed, unless and until Congress finds a way to make these politically difficult decisions with some degree of protection against political fallout.

In recent years, our government has developed such a technique. It's called a bipartisan commission, a joint enterprise of both Democrats and Republicans that forces both sides to share the political burden of unpopular decisions, minimizes the risk of political vulnerability for any individual representative, and enables elected officials to collaborate closely with preeminent experts and civic leaders. Commissions designed on this model have already produced constructive results in a variety of areas.

For example, early in the Reagan administration, when Social Security was heading dangerously close to the brink of insolvency and neither Congress nor the President was willing to take the blame for the difficult steps needed, they convened the bipartisan Greenspan Commission, which resulted in the 1983 amendments to the Social Security Act that placed the system on a firmer footing with a package of payroll tax hikes and phased-in benefit reductions. When deficits were raging out of control in 1988 despite the Gramm-Rudman-Hollings legislation, and the hardball politics of a presidential campaign season prevented rational solutions from even being debated, I proposed and the Congress enacted a bipartisan National Economic Commission to present options to the incoming President; unfortunately, President-elect Bush undermined the commission's work —a shortsighted decision that contributed to his political downfall, as Bush officials later conceded.

More recently, tight budgets and the end of the Cold War made it necessary to close hundreds of military bases, but the job looked impossible because each member of Congress was bound to protect every base in his or her district. In response, Congress established a bipartisan Base Closure and Realignment Commission, which has completed three painful but necessary rounds of base closings. Similarly, with the public demanding campaign and lobbying reform, but with incumbents of both parties reluctant to give up the advantages the current system gives them and afraid to bite the hand of the special interests who feed them campaign money, Speaker Gingrich and the President recently agreed upon a bipartisan commission to develop viable proposals for reform. And Senate Majority Leader Bob Dole has already indicated interest in a new bipartisan commission to rescue Medicare in a manner that would continue to assure affordable health care for the elderly while controlling the explosive growth in costs.

Of course it would be better if our senators and representatives would simply stand up and commit publicly to the tough decisions they currently talk about only in the privacy of their parlors, even if it jeopardized their political futures. But that's not going to happen. So why not use a strategy that the Speaker of the House, the Majority Leader of the Senate, and the President have all agreed on before? Why not set up a bipartisan commission on Medicare? And if that commission succeeds, as surely it could, we could then launch a second commission to tackle Social Security, federal civilian and military retirement, and other entitlements. What do we have to lose?

In sum, if we want to grow economically, we need to find ways to boost public investment without increasing the deficit. That means cutting lower-priority spending and restraining the growth in entitlements. The chief principle in budget cutting must be: programs to meet our needs, not our wants. Cuts may be painful, so they must be administered in moderation; too radical a surgery might kill the patient. With tactics like these, we've already made progress in reducing the deficit. The important thing is to continue on that path. And if a bipartisan commission is the only way, by all means let's do it.

Honest, Effective Government

We cannot hope to make much progress on any front, from jobs to crime to illegitimacy, until we do one other thing first. We need to convince the people they can trust their government again.

When asked if "government always manages to mess things up," two-thirds of Americans answer yes. The average American believes we waste 48 cents of every tax dollar. Until we change these perceptions, the national conversation we need to begin about shared sacrifice and national community will be difficult.

To move us toward a spirit of greater public confidence, we should make a major commitment to enacting campaign finance and lobbying reform. The first and most important step: reducing the influence of money in campaigns. The average cost for a House seat now exceeds $550,000. For a Senate seat, it's $3.6 million. The representatives we elect to serve our interests and to deliberate over our policies and laws now typically spend more than half their time fund-raising, showing up at the cocktail

parties of big-money lobbyists and calling wealthy contributors.
They do it because they have to; they know how much it costs
to win a race. But the side effects are unacceptable. Not only are
they wasting time better spent on making policy, but they are
fostering the suspicion that all these contributions buy, if not
votes, then at least an unfair degree of access.

One of the culprits is the double evil of high-priced TV and
radio advertising. The need to advertise on television is the single
biggest factor driving up the costs of campaigning. At the same
time, the ads that money pays for are reducing the majesty of
our democracy to a battle of warring thirty-second sound bites
that are about as enlightening as the unending battle of the
long-distance phone companies for our attention and credulity.
Another culprit is the excessive—and constantly expanding—
length of the campaign season, which makes campaigning a
financial as well as a physical endurance test.

We need to find sensible and constitutionally permissible
ways of limiting both the demand for and the supply of campaign money. Basically, that means limiting how much candidates spend on campaigns and what they receive in
contributions. We need to do both, because if you limit the flow
of campaign funds from any one source—like corporate gifts
or personal wealth—without curbing the astronomical costs of
campaigning, politicians serious about winning will have no
choice but to redouble their efforts to find new loopholes and
new sources. One way to limit both costs and contributions
would be to impose voluntary caps on both: candidates would
accept the caps in exchange for public financing and access to
free or less expensive airtime. We would also need to make sure
that such broadcast access was geared to in-depth debates and
presentations rather than thirty-second commercials that package candidates like so much soap.

The other key is to take stronger steps to limit the influence
of lobbyists. We should ban them from giving gifts to elected
officials and bar the officials from accepting them. And to make
sure that the public has a chance to know what their representatives are being told by paid representatives of industry, we

should force lobbyists not only to register themselves officially but to report, in detail, the subject of their contacts with government officials.

Democrats say they are eager to make these changes, but one can't help noticing that they didn't when they had the chance to. Similarly, Republicans made reform a rhetorical priority—when they were out of power. But now that they are in control of Congress—and raking in record campaign contributions from the special interests—they don't want to kill the goose that now lays golden eggs for them. Big ones!

Maybe we've become so accustomed to this kind of hypocrisy we've lost our interest in changing it. That would be a mistake. We should remember two things: First, this is *our* government, unless we give it away. And second, these days, the people in office will do anything we demand of them if we demand it loudly and long enough; it's up to us to speak out.

And it's up to us to put our votes where our mouths are. Barely half of eligible voters bother to vote for President; as few as one-third participate in congressional elections. If everyone who is eligible voted, it just might change the face of politics. It would almost certainly change many of the faces in office. Maybe that's why those already in office are so insistent about maintaining all the current impediments to voting. They rationalize their fear of change by insisting that the future of our democracy somehow depends on voters registering weeks in advance and voting all on the same day and in person.

What if you could register when you went to the polls to vote? What if "Election Day" lasted a week, or at least was switched from Tuesdays to Saturdays and Sundays? What if we gave everyone, not just those away from home, the option of voting by mail? I think these changes would lead to a stronger, more vibrant democracy.

As for the unelected portion of the government, we should insist that agencies be as productive, responsive, and results-oriented as we can make them. Wherever possible, we should build the idea of measuring performance and outcomes into the design or redesign of every program. That's what Vice President

Gore's Reinventing Government effort is all about, and it's working well.

The answer to making government work better, however, is not to disparage it, much less dismantle it. During the Reagan era, for example, the President himself led the chorus of disrespect in disparaging government workers. People were appointed to head agencies whose mission they were fundamentally opposed to, as when James Watt was charged with guarding our natural resources or now–Supreme Court Justice Clarence Thomas was put in charge of the Equal Employment Opportunity Commission.

But for all government's faults and foibles, we should resist the temptation to follow leaders who encourage us to throw up our hands in disgust or turn our backs on the idea of community. Instead, we should rededicate ourselves to honing the tools of government—tools that we the people can use to build an American future on a firm foundation of economic prosperity and social justice. In the end, the last, best hope for our national community is that the people will decide they once more have the patience to play another inning in the magnificent, ramshackle ballpark of our democracy.

6

Something Real to
Believe In

Like deciphering the earth itself, trying to understand America's current political condition requires us to study its different layers.

At the surface where we walk, work, worry, and wonder, there are dozens of dilemmas and opportunities that we deal with daily. They express themselves in today's familiar litany of news show topics and headline stories: How do we cut the deficit? How do we create an economy that is good for middle-class American workers and not just owners and investors? What do we do about the social catastrophes—the drugs, crime, violence, institutionalized poverty—that have created a dejected second city where the glitter of the City on the Hill does not show? We argue over the morality of abortion, the side effects of welfare regulations, the merits of punishment, the obligation to protect our environment. We debate whether it's enough to "send a message to the irresponsible" or whether we have to send some opportunity as well. We try to decide whether Washington should turn some of the biggest problems over to the individual states, even though the last time we tried it, with the Articles of Confederation, it failed so badly we had to invent the Constitution to save ourselves from chaos.

Even if we set aside the tangled questions of our proper role in international episodes of savagery and slaughter like Bosnia, our lives are full of immediate concerns and the need for quick decisions. Some of us try to stay engaged with these questions, but most of us don't, because we don't have the time, or because we feel so remote from the power to make a difference that we don't see the point of trying.

Even fewer of us are given the chance to explore the forces beneath the surface, the historic developments that produced and help explain these daily challenges. The fantastic explosion of technological capacities. Globalization. The weakening of labor unions. Our gradual decline from world economic dominance. How we slipped because of the erosion of our own will and discipline, while our competitors—former enemies we helped rebuild—charged forward with the same hunger to achieve and prevail that fueled our own triumph in World War II and the years immediately after it. The invasion of heroin in the 1960s and the concomitant rise in violence and alienation as we entered the thirty-year war of drugs against sanity.

In an easier world we would all have the time we need to study that history, with its syndromes, fads, cycles, and implicit suggestions as to how to do things better the next time.

But even then, if we did not probe a little deeper in our exploration, we would still be overlooking something—perhaps the most compelling truth of all. Accumulating deep below, drifting up between the cracks, insinuating itself into our consciousness, is a sense that there's something missing. The political answers seem too shallow, too shortsighted, too harsh. There must be something deeper, grander, stronger—even sweeter perhaps—that can help us deal with our problems by making us better than we are . . . instead of meaner. That can lift our aspirations instead of lowering them. All around us is the feeling that we will not progress as we should if all we manage is the superficial manipulation of our day-to-day inconveniences. Surely we will not be able to achieve the better society we hope for by deliberately increasing our fragmentation, disintegration, alienation, and hostility.

We feel this hunger for larger answers as a vague ache of uncertainty and dissatisfaction. We play around with words that hint at it—"values," "character," occasionally even "morality." We see it suggested in the growing affection for some kind of religious thinking that will help us answer the plaintive cries of recent years and show us where indeed Joe DiMaggio has gone. We see it in the yearning for something to fill the vacuum that has disconcerted us increasingly over the last fifty years: no great hero or heroine, no uplifting cause, no reassuring orthodoxy or stimulating new rationale.

That is where we should start our search for meaningful answers. Give me something real to live by, to live for, something bigger than myself alone. Because for all my personal fears, for all the energy I put into the struggle for my own survival and that of my family—I know in the end that I am not enough for me.

Momma knew that truth. She knew it without polls, which, after all, mostly just measure our confusion. She knew it with a wisdom more subtle than computers or macroeconomic modeling and more perceptive than even the most exquisite of our political punditry. And she taught it indelibly—the way Poppa and my wife, Matilda's, parents did—by the quiet, magnificent example of her own life and the occasional stunning power of her simple words. One day in the late 1930s, she was giving scraps of food from our little grocery store to a Gypsy woman and her children, when one of our Italian customers—a laborer, callused and bent by the pick, the shovel, and the wheelbarrow —asked her in angry tones, "Why do you give that to them free when we have to pay?" Momma's answer came in her rough, uneven Italian, but it was this: "Because she's hungry and she's doing all she can do for herself. Because she's like me. That's why I give her bread to eat. Why do you question that?"

This book began with Momma and it will end with her, because her story tells us something about America that we are being invited to forget. The immigrant saga my parents lived could be exploited as a perfect conservative Republican parable, notwithstanding the inconvenient coda of my own political ca-

reer. "See? They came from nothing, nothing, not even a boot-
strap between them, and they lifted themselves up the
old-fashioned way: nothing but grit and hard work and ambition,
and no help from anyone!"

That my parents survived at all in this country was indeed a
breathtaking achievement. That they succeeded as they did is
still a dazzling thing. Yes, they worked incredibly hard, both of
them, around the clock every day for decades. They sacrificed
themselves for their children in a way that sounds almost implau-
sible today. All of that is true. But it would be wrong to say they
did it all by themselves.

Momma was born in a part of rural Italy where there was
essentially no government—where, in fact, there was very little
of anything. I have sometimes described it as a farm, although
she would have resisted that title as being too good for a place
that had no way to get water except from the rain. From the dust
of that hillside her family somehow coaxed a living, but it was
the kind of grinding endless struggle that encourages an enthusi-
astic belief in a next world sweeter than this one. There were no
schools, no electricity, not a paved road for fifty miles. Life was
conducted on the frontier of desperation in a village ignored
almost entirely by the larger society beyond. When she met a
young man with a strong back but no money, and he asked her
to marry him and go to America, the only available answer
was yes.

And so in the early part of the twentieth century, they came
and found an America that was just beginning to think of itself
in a new way. Even before the country woke up in a daze in the
dungeon of the Great Depression, America was already awake
to the idea that promoting the national interest could mean more
than watching a dozen families get remarkably rich. The populists, the progressives, the new labor movement, and even some
establishment politicians and business leaders had begun to
think we could and should do more for one another through our
government than we had for our first century. When the door
finally clanged shut and the Depression trapped us all together
inside, those ideas were what saved the country.

Momma didn't come here for what our government offered,

but she couldn't have stayed without it. Without the jobs created by FDR's Works Progress Administration, she and Poppa would have had to close our tiny grocery store for lack of customers; most of the neighborhood would have been out of work. Without the unfailing patience of the teachers at Public School 50, none of her three children would ever have learned English, much less how to read. Without Queens General Hospital, the broken bones of our growing up would actually have gone unset. Frankly, without a government committed to the advancement of our common good, Momma would have gotten back on the boat and I'd be stuck on a rock on a hill in Salerno, praying for rain.

In the end though, my mother's story really belongs to all of us. The signers of the Contract would like us to forget the hundred ways that government provides the help, healing, and protection we all need. No matter what they say, however, it's still the case that anyone who ever went to a state college, drove on a public highway, checked a book out of a community library, got a polio vaccine, or even drank a glass of pasteurized milk in this country has been climbing a ladder of opportunity that none of us built ourselves and that private enterprise would not have guaranteed us.

We are being told by the people who have recently come to power that we should abandon that course now—that it is bad for us. And they are on the verge of enshrining that abandonment in law. I count it almost a mercy that my mother will not have to witness the hour when America walks out on sixty years of the most humane and intelligent progress any government has ever achieved, because the nation was seduced by a new mythology that insists the strongest among us are sufficient unto themselves and the rest are not worth the bother.

It is a faithlessness that defies the compelling evidence all around us. Never have there been more ways of measuring our interdependence: A securities scandal in a distant capital rattles markets around the world in less than an hour. My prudent downsizing is your brutal layoff. Your local war is our oil crisis. Our thriving factories are the acid rain of your dying lakes. My lack of health insurance is your soaring premium. Your cruel sweatshop is my bargain sportswear. My federal tax break is your local tax hike. Your cigarette is my lung disease. Surely the connections are not too faint to trace.

At the moment, however, rather than facing the implications of our intertwining fates, we are turning our gaze to conjurers eager to persuade us that our obligations in the world end at our own front door.

What would Momma have said? She would have told us that such talk was foolishness, and that now—when our problems are so large—is surely not the time for us to quit trying to make a better world for one another.

But no matter what she might have said, the proposition that we should be free of obligations to each other surely remains tempting, strongly tempting, at least to some of us. Today's radical Republicans understand that temptation so well they have built their revolution on it. "Look," they say, "the poor, the addicted, the desperate, the people in the crumbling cities, the fifty-year-old workers just downsized our of their dignity and hope—those people are practically doomed. But don't worry. You're fit, you're fortunate, and those people are not your responsibility. Frankly, you'll be doing them a favor if you just give up and walk away. It might teach them to look after themselves."

That's quite an invitation, especially for someone like me, who is already comfortable in life and who is much more than halfway home. Someone lucky enough to have moved away from the old struggling neighborhood and who would prefer to believe that its troubles are no longer mine.

After all, even the worst of our common problems won't catch me in my lifetime. I can move away from the crime. Medicare and Social Security will still be there when I need them. The riots of fury and despair won't come soon enough to threaten me. And if we eliminated the Environmental Protection Agency tomorrow, the fish and the forests would live long enough to accommodate my desires.

The signers of the Contract tempt me and other fortunate Americans with all the luxuries of individualism and indifference to the wider world. So why not simply give in?

Why not? Frankly, because I find the invitation of the Contract offensive. How dare they prey on our fears and frustration! How dare they behave as if we won't notice the evasion and simplistics! How dare they think so little of us and what we're capable of!

I reject the invitation also because I don't want to leave behind me an America that is not as good as the one I was given. Because I'm humiliated to think that my children and theirs would inherit a shrunken, desiccated vision of what this place can be, withered in opportunity and quality of life, diminished in justice, hope, and aspiration. I reject it because I cannot face the idea that mine would be the first generation of Americans in our modern history who failed to see that our immediate convenience was not necessarily identical with the nation's greatest good.

The new leaders of our legislative branch say they, too, are concerned with the great legacy we have inherited. In fact, they would like us to believe that all the charts we need to guide our majestic, magnificently complicated ship of state were laid out for us by the Founding Fathers.

With all due respect to the geniuses who first shaped this miracle of a nation, the wisdom of their day was designed to govern a society in which the only people who counted fully as people were landowning, white, Christian men. It is a wisdom we need to govern our own time—but it is not wisdom enough.

As they shaped a new nation, the Founders were exploring the possibilities of a brand-new intellectual prism we now call individualism. It was and is a thing of thrilling power. Pass the American people through that prism and we break up into a magnificent rainbow: 250 million wavelengths unfurled. Seeing it for the first time in history, the Founders thought it was beautiful, and they were right. But we need to remember today that it is only one way of seeing the shaft of light that shines down on this extraordinary place: America is also and equally the bright, warm sunlight in which the colors and differences come together as one. We are also a community—and we must also value that.

Yes, we should remember our past—but remember all of it. We should remember that, in just two hundred years, we invented a society—and saved it from shattering. We defeated the greatest armies mankind ever raised. We have opened our gates and our hearts to ten generations of seekers from every corner of the earth, and made democracy work better than anyone dreamed it could. How? By being honest. Bold. Courageous. And positive. By being better than our worst impulses. And by being more, together, than any of us could have been alone. During World War II, throughout the battles for worker protection and public education and Social Security and civil rights, whenever we have been at our very best, we have succeeded, when we might have failed, by recognizing that we have an obligation to one another. Not just because it's a nice idea, but because we need everyone helping to pull the wagon.

We still do. It is a simple truth our hearts already know: we cannot reach the levels of strength and civility we should with one-third of our people striding up the mountain with perfect confidence, one-third desperate in the ditches by the side of the trail, and the third in between wondering whether they'll slip down into the ditch themselves.

We have an opportunity now to make progress such as we have not seen in decades, inspired by a new and richer American Dream. We can create a nation stronger, wiser, and sweeter than it has ever been. But it can only be done together. Momma understood that. So should we.

Acknowledgments

In the effort to get this book in print, I relied on a familiar cast of friends and colleagues, but several of the most important faces were new. I am profoundly grateful to Alice Mayhew of Simon & Schuster for the insight that there was a book here to be written and for the frankness and intelligence that helped me find the sculpture in the stone; and to Jim Griffin at William Morris, who helped me find Alice in the wonderful world of publishing.

The book would not have been the same without the assistance of two talented, indefatigable, and highly disciplined professionals, both of whom worked with me previously in state government, Steve Hoffman and Martha Eddison. Both of them helped me analyze the issues and clarify my vision of how we should deal with them, and Steve served as a vigorous in-house devil's advocate as well. His recent role was only one in which he has excelled over all the years I've known him, as a lawyer, lobbyist, political analyst, writer, researcher, and even as a disc jockey specializing in the blues. Martha is a highly intelligent, passionate humanist and a gifted writer with a flair for metaphors that can make the most arcane analysis accessible. Someday I hope Steve and Martha will write their own books so their intelligence and sensitivity will come directly to America's readers.

Jason Halperin, Elizabeth Starkey, and Sandra Cuneo have my gratitude for the sound advice they offered so generously. Thanks also to Jennifer Collesano for her research assistance and Stacey Davis for her help with the typing.

I cannot find words to describe adequately my profound gratitude to my family. I am humbled by their patience, generosity, and willingness to help with all my public work, including this book. Thank you Margaret, Andrew, Maria, Madeline, Christopher, Howard, Kerry, Kenneth, and Brian. And thank you for the six jewels that give our family new sparkle: Christina, Emily, Amanda, Catherine, Cara, and Mariah.

The crown jewel, of course, is my wife, Matilda. Without her there would be no family and no book. I may never understand how Matilda keeps finding a way to forgive the infuriating habits of a lifetime, including my continuing tendency to work as if it were still my sworn duty to do so.

I dedicate this book and the years of work it represents to all of them: to Momma, Pop, Matilda's mother and father, Mary and Charles Raffa, and in a special way to my brother and sister, Frank and Marie, for their lifetime of goodness and grace.

Index

—